Acknowledgments

We would like to express our appreciation to the following for their editorial and technical assistance:

James Andrews, Lauren Elkin, Menachem Mendel Feller, Mindelle Feller, Sara Leah Krinsky, Adel Panzer Morris, Leah Naster.

Special advisors, Stu Abraham, John Kudrle, Harry Lerner, John McHugh, Dick Newman, Robert Rachlin, Norton Stillman, Dennis Trainor, and David Wexler.

At Harper San Francisco, John Loudon, senior editor, and Georgia Hughes, senior editorial assistant.

At Community Education Organization, Aarah Aizman, Jeffrey Dehler, Mordechai Dorfman, Max Elkin, Miriam Leah Frank, Shlomo Friedman, Yochonon Friedman, Eli Greenspan, Herschel Gruenberg, Berkeh Mishulovin, Yoni Morris, Chana Rosenthal, Mordechai Rosenthal, Sholom Mordechai Rubashkin, Gerald Sadoff, Jean Sadoff, Eric Simon and Tzivia Leah Tarshish.

With grateful recognition to Agri-Processors of Iowa, Old City Foods, and Shafer & Feld Printers for their generous support.

Introduction

Manis Friedman has been called a modern-day Will Rogers. His phenomenal popularity and appeal can be explained by a Hebrew word that I expect will soon become part of the everyday vocabulary of America. The word is *maggid*.

Traditionally, a *maggid* was a roving preacher of eastern Europe. He spoke to simple folk in plain everyday language, a delightful contrast to the more formal rabbinic scholars of the day. The *maggid* wove together legends, songs, parables, and jokes. He gathered a crowd wherever he stopped, inspiring them in a way that no stern-faced scholar could.

Today Friedman carries on the tradition, giving it new life and meaning. He travels from city to city, sometimes speaking in as many as three a week, all over the world. Wherever he speaks there is always a crowd mesmerized by his stories, his humor, his mixture of American slang and poetry, and his deeply inspiring message.

I first saw and heard Friedman in his role as *maggid* in December of 1987, while attending a private conference at the Crown Palace Hotel in New York City. I had heard Friedman teach at his school, Bais Chana Institute in Minnesota, and I was curious to see and hear him in a different setting. I was completely unprepared for what I experienced.

Friedman was scheduled to speak the second night of the conference. Since the conference sessions weren't open to the public, there had been no general publicity. No news releases, no letters, no announcements, none of the usual notices had gone out stating that Friedman was in town or was scheduled to speak. According to the conference rules, only those registered ought to have attended, and there were about seventy of us. So when I arrived at the last minute I was startled to find the lecture hall filled with hundreds of people. Fortunately, a friend of mine had saved me a seat.

"Who are all these people?" I asked.

My friend laughed. "Oh, they come from all over New York."

"What are they doing here?" I could see that the halls and doorways were filled with people still arriving.

"This always happens when he comes to New York. Everyone wants to hear him."

"How do they find out?"

"Word of mouth, I guess. News travels quickly."

By now there was no room left in the lecture hall. People were packed shoulder to shoulder in every available inch of space—a fire marshall's nightmare. No one seemed to mind standing, and the crowd was polite, quiet, and patient, in spite of the fact that there was barely room to breathe.

At last Friedman arrived. A small, trim man in his early forties, he was dressed in an elegant knee-length Prince Albert coat, the traditional Sabbath attire of a Lubavitcher Chasidic Jew.

When he spoke his voice was soft. Although he used no microphone, he could be heard in the farthest corners of the room. As he spoke he rocked from one foot to the other, keeping time with the rhythm of his speech.

His listeners were spellbound. He spoke for about an hour, then the audience kept him for another hour with a constant stream of questions. The message was simple and often funny—humor is his trademark—and this modern-day *maggid* touched the hearts of all those present.

Later, I learned that when the halls of the hotel could contain no more people, the management locked the front doors. Nevertheless, people continued to wait outside, in New York in the middle of December, hoping for a chance to hear Manis Friedman of Minnesota speak in person.

Since that December evening, as Friedman's reputation has continued to grow, so has the global demand for his appearances, especially during the spring and fall months when Bais Chana Institute is not in session. In a typical year he speaks to packed houses in Chicago, Los Angeles, Hong Kong, Toronto, London, and Vancouver. Recently he was invited to England to speak at Oxford University, and was interviewed live over the BBC Radio Network.

California journalist Jay Gordon has written, "Manis Friedman is acclaimed as a most gifted and perceptive lecturer who often leads his audiences through captivating expeditions exploring the very core and soul of Judaism. His broad command of philosophical and mystical Jewish concepts, his ability to elucidate these concepts in practical terms, and to relate them to challenging contemporary issues, are appreciated by scholar and layman alike. He is considered one of the foremost exponents of traditional Jewish philosophy today."

Friedman was born in 1946 in Prague, Czechoslovakia, and immigrated to the United States with his family in 1950. He began working for the Lubavitch Youth Organization as a public speaker in 1964. In 1969 he was ordained at the Lubavitch Rabbinical College of Canada, and soon after joined the Upper Midwest Merkos Lubavitch as director of its Student Outreach Program.

In 1971 Friedman cofounded, with Rabbi and Mrs. Moshe Feller, Bais Chana Institute of Jewish Studies in Minnesota. Located in a stone mansion on a tree-lined street in residential St. Paul, this unique learning center has been called the "pet project" of US Senator Rudy Boschwitz (R) of Minnesota.

In the summer of 1988, I attended one of Friedman's classes at Bais Chana, held on the second floor in a library-turned-classroom. Demand for his teachings was so great that over eighty students were packed inside a room designed to hold forty. Outside it was 97 degrees. Inside, it was nearly as hot. In this sweltering, crowded room students from Argentina, Australia, Brazil, Canada, Egypt, England, France, Israel, Italy, Portugal, Russia, and the United States were sitting together, intently listening. Friedman spoke to this rapt audience for nearly four hours. It was a typical daily class.

What drew those people to Bais Chana that summer? Partly, it was the desire to return to the traditions of their forebears. But a more compelling reason was the wish to study personally with Manis Friedman. Over the past eighteen years the Institute has attracted nearly six thousand students from a wide variety of backgrounds and from every corner of the globe. In his classes at Bais Chana and in his lectures given around the world, Friedman teaches the relevance of immortal Jewish wisdom to our everyday lives.

Cassette recordings of Friedman's most popular lectures were first reproduced by a staff of volunteers in the basement of the Institute in 1985; they immediately began selling at the rate of several hundred copies a month. To date over 75,000 tapes have been sold, mostly through word of mouth.

In the fall of 1989 a series of lectures by Friedman entitled "Torah Forum," videotaped before live audiences, was televised on Twin Cities Regional Cable Network. The series, now carried on cable stations throughout the United States and Canada, met with intense critical acclaim. It was named "Critic's Choice" by the *Minneapolis Star Tribune;* called "erudite and provocative" by *Mpls. St. Paul* magazine; and termed "a consuming experience" by the *St. Paul Pioneer Press/Dispatch.*

The ever-increasing demand for Friedman's lectures, both in person and on tape, led to the inception of this book. The essays in this book are based on several lectures selected for their fresh and provocative content, as well as the strong response to each by enthusiastic audiences. The lectures have been edited and expanded for the printed page—Friedman's unique speaking style, his wit, his wisdom, and his solid, down-to-earth, make-sense answers carefully preserved.

Manis Friedman is a dynamic and charismatic teacher. He has a special quality that enables him to touch the hearts of people across the broad spectrum of modern life. And his message is both startlingly new and powerfully ancient.

The central theme of this book is modesty, a notion so simple and common that most of us would dismiss it as irrelevant to our daily lives. But Friedman asks us to look again. And as we do he explains, clearly and succinctly, how modesty can become a powerful tool for change.

Gently and with humor, he helps us redirect our thinking about sexuality and refocus our ideas about intimacy. In so doing, he moves us toward a truer understanding of ourselves and how we can cope with the changing world around us. His words give us a new understanding of the moral foundations upon which intimacy, modesty, and sexuality depend.

JS Morris, Editor
Bais Chana Tapes
December 17, 1989

Prologue: Borders

A wealthy benefactor once came to visit a hospital he supported. As he entered the building, he saw — to his horror — a mouse. "This is terrible!" he cried. "Shut the entire hospital down right away."

An emergency meeting of the board was called. The board members sat, talked, discussed and debated for hours. Finally they turned to the chief of staff and said, "What do you think?"

The administrator answered as follows:

"It says in the Bible that God created every creature with its borders. Certain creatures live on dry land, certain creatures live in jungles. Some live in swamps, some in high places, and others in low places. But every creature has its borders.

"Even in time, there are borders. Certain creatures work at night and sleep during the day. Others sleep during the day and work at night. Some are active during the summer, others during the winter. These are the different borders in time.

"This is even referred to in the Book of Psalms, where it's written that the sun sets and the animals come out to do their work. When the sun comes up, the animals go back to their hiding places and the people come out. So every creature has its borders in time and space, and its definition as to what it's supposed to do.

"Now it happened that one crazy mouse got confused and wandered away from its border. It trespassed onto the border of human beings. Therefore, nine businessmen left their businesses to come here today and sit around and discuss what should be done with a single mouse who got lost!"

The chief of staff sat down again. Feeling silly, the nine trustees called off the meeting and went home.

* * * * *

The ancient sages taught that there are four basic kinds of people. The first person says, "What's mine is mine and what's yours is mine." This kind of person is wicked and selfish.

The second says, "What's mine is yours and what's yours is yours." This is a generous person, a saintly person, a person to be admired.

The third says, "What's yours is yours and what's mine is mine." Not too generous but not too selfish either.

And the fourth says, "What's mine is yours and what's yours is mine." The sages called this kind of person an ignoramus.

If what's mine is mine and what's yours is mine, then I want everything. If what's mine is yours and what's yours is yours, then you can have everything. If mine is mine and yours is yours, then you can have what's yours and I'll have what's mine.

But if mine is yours and yours is mine, what in the world is that? It's a free-for-all, the opposite of a stable and orderly society.

We say, "I'll take whatever I feel like taking, and you take whatever you feel like taking. What's mine is not mine, what's yours is not yours." Which means, "I'm not me and you're not you." It's insanity, but it's the way we live our lives all too often.

When the Children of Israel came into the Promised Land, the first miracle that happened was the fall of the walls of Jericho. After that, complete victory was certain. Once the walls fell, it was all over. What was inside was theirs for the taking.

When the borders of the world fall, when the walls of morality fall, everything falls. To have no borders at all is to live with insecurity.

It used to be that the borders of the world were very clear. Day was day, night was night, good was good and bad was bad. Today the whole world is suffering from a pervasive loss of borders.

Global borders have all but disappeared. In the past, when a nation wanted to wage war, its army would cross a border to invade another nation's territory. Today they don't cross a border at all; a commander can sit at home, push a button, and wipe out a country three thousand miles away. ·

xviii

Even the human body no longer recognizes its borders. Disease used to be something that came from outside and attacked the body. Today's diseases are from within the body itself. Either the body suddenly develops tissue where it's not supposed to, or destroys parts of itself that it shouldn't be destroying.

AIDS is a perfect example of a lack of borders: The immune system has gone berserk and the body no longer knows how to defend itself. When the body is so confused about itself, it's a loss of borders.

The loss of borders even threatens to destroy families. Family life used to be a very strong border. A person's family was like a little world unto itself. There was a border that set the family territory apart from the non-family, what was private from what was public. Family was family; home was home.

The family borders were maintained: strong, healthy, clear, and unquestioned. They were based on loyalty, respect, and trust. Today those borders are weakened and blurred, even in the best of families. As a result, family life is suffering.

A family border is like the skin of a balloon. When holes are poked in a balloon, the air escapes. If a breach in a family border occurs, the love dissipates.

Children used to know they'd come home and find their mother and father there. Now it's not so certain. Today, children leave for school wondering whether they'll come home to find that one or both of their parents will have abandoned them.

In our personal lives, our feelings no longer have borders. We've lost touch with ourselves and become confused. Are we in love or just infatuated? Are we angry or vaguely uneasy? Are we upset or perfectly fine? We don't know anymore.

We're left with no borders for ourselves as individuals, no definitions, no sense of selfhood. If we allow people to take advantage of us, if we allow people to hurt us, if we allow people to walk all over us, it's because we have no borders.

We're taught to build up our self-esteem, and so we tell ourselves: "I'm smart, I'm good looking, I'm talented, I'm wonderful." Then we start believing it: "Maybe I am a little bit special. I'm not so stupid after all." And then, "You're right; I can have it my way. I ought to have it my way, and nobody is going to tell me what to do. I deserve it all."

Suddenly, we're monsters. We don't let people step on us anymore; we step on them first. Again, it's because we have no borders. Emotionally we feel, "I can't wait until tomorrow to express myself, I have to do it now. If you don't want to listen, you're not really my friend."

We're out of control; we have no limits on our own emotions. And we were taught to be that way as children. Our parents told us, "All we're interested in is your happiness." Now that we're adults, we run around saying, "It's my time to express myself," even though no one is interested, no one wants to hear and everyone is in a completely different mood.

I was visiting an Alcoholics Anonymous meeting once when a woman recounted a tragic story about how her husband's drunken driving had nearly killed their children. She smiled as she spoke. When the counselor pointed out to her that smiling at such a time was inappropriate, she excused it by saying, "I can't seem to help it." The counselor told her, "That's what your husband says about his drinking: he can't help it; he just 'has to.'"

When we have borders, we express our feelings only when it's appropriate and do not express them when it isn't. We do not impose ourselves on others.

When we have no borders, the way we conduct our lives depends on how we feel at the time. That's not sanity; that creates insecurity. But thinking well of ourselves won't make us feel more secure. We will feel secure when we know what we ought to be doing.

There's an old saying, "Don't laugh at a funeral or cry at a wedding." In different words, it means: "Establish borders with your feelings and your behavior."

You might say, "I'm an honest person. When I'm sad, I'm sad. What am I supposed to do, make believe I'm happy? I'm too virtuous for that."

Well, even honesty has its borders. There are times when your sadness, your happiness, and your honesty are all irrelevant - for example, at a funeral. At someone else's funeral, expressing your happiness is totally inappropriate and unwelcome, out of its border.

At someone else's wedding, you're supposed to do what they expect you to do, what they need you to do, and that is dance and enjoy. Don't say, "But I'm the honest type," because no one is talking about you right now. It's not your wedding. Even if it were, you shouldn't cry. You invited guests who came to celebrate. If you start crying, you're out of line. Being out of line means not recognizing borders.

If we have nothing that says our life is described by certain limits, that we may live within these borders, that we may not live outside those borders, then we have no borders except our own egos.

When God created the world, it was part of His plan to give everything a limit, everything its borders. By giving us borders, God gave us a true sense of security, not through artificial self-esteem or unlimited ego but through morality.

If we know what we may do and what we may not do, then we have borders. Then we have a clear idea of what is appropriate and what is inappropriate; what is allowed and what is not allowed; what is right and what is wrong.

There is one border that makes us who we are more than any other: modesty. Modesty is the framework that gives us a sense of self and a blueprint for stability.

We know that God wants modesty because He Himself is modest. It is part of God's modesty that He even limited how far He revealed Himself to the world, containing Himself to a certain degree. He limited how much energy He put into the world, and how long the world will exist.

When God decided to dwell on earth among human beings, He wanted to do so in modesty. According to Jewish mysticism, the relationship between God and mankind is a marriage, a very modest marriage from which we learn how much God cherishes modesty.

The purpose for which the Holy Temple was built in Jerusalem was to contain God's Presence, called in Hebrew the "Shekhinah," the feminine aspect of God. The structure of the Temple itself resembled a womb. God is referred to as He, and the Holy Temple as She; God is called our Father, the Temple our Mother.

The parallel to a marriage between a man and a woman is carried through most of the laws pertaining to the Holy Temple. For example, a man is not allowed to lie with his wife if one of them is drunk; a priest was not allowed to enter the Temple if he was drunk.

God told King Solomon, "Build Me a house that I can dwell in it. Make me a fence, and within the fence, make me a courtyard. Within the courtyard, build me a building, with walls. And within those walls, there have to be rooms. And within those rooms, there have to be partitions and doors. And on those doors, you must hang for Me curtains."

For this to be God's house, there had to be a curtain on the door to the courtyard, a curtain on the door to the Temple, and a curtain on the door to the chambers within.

In the Holy Temple, there were two chambers, the inner chamber and the outer chamber. The outer chamber was called "Holy". The inner chamber, the dwelling place of God's Presence, was called the "Holy of Holies". The difference between the two chambers was that although every priest could enter the outer chamber, only one was chosen to become the High Priest, and only he could enter the Holy of Holies.

Between the Holy and the Holy of Holies there was also a curtain. All of these curtains represented God's modesty, because even God needs borders.

Only one man was allowed to enter the Holy of Holies, and that was the High Priest. So the question is asked: If something needed repairing, what could they do? If the walls cracked, they would need to be repaired. If no one was allowed to enter the Holy of Holies, how could this be done?

Above the Holy of Holies was yet another chamber, from which a basket could be lowered with a workman inside. The basket was closed on three sides, and open only on the side of the wall that needed to be mended. The workman could do what he needed to do, repair what needed to be repaired, yet remain closed off from the rest of the room.

This special chamber above the Holy of Holies was called the "Bedroom," even though there were no beds in it.

The "Holy" represents the state of innocence that a woman is in before she is married. The "Holy of Holies" is the state of being married, a state of even greater sanctification which is shared with only one person, just as only one priest, the High Priest, could enter the inner chamber. Before a woman is married, there are many possibilities as to whom she may marry, but after she is married, there is only one man whom she has chosen.

Between the two chambers was a curtain. In the parallel to marriage, the curtain represents the veil with which a bride covers her face and hair.

As in the Holy Temple, God expects us to live with clearly defined borders in our lives. Modesty is the one border that stands out above all the others. Both the curtain and the bridal veil represent modesty. Just as the curtain separated the outer chamber, which was public, from the inner chamber, which was private, the bridal veil distinguishes between a single woman and a married woman.

The Holy of Holies contained the ark which held the tablets of the Ten Commandments, the essence of God's Holy Scripture. Above the Ark, there was the chamber mentioned before, the "Bedroom".

In marriage there are also two parts. There is the part which corresponds to Scripture, that is, the marriage vows, the sacred institution of marriage. And there is the physical relationship, the intimacy of marriage, which is considered even higher.

From this, we have a very clear definition, very clear borders, as to what our lives are to consist of. First there is the state of being single, when we are to be modest and holy, then the state of being married, when our sanctity and our modesty increases. The bedroom, the intimacy of marriage, is the highest state of all, because from this room came the power to repair the walls of the Temple itself.

The message for us is clear: If our lives are not quite right today, if our relationships need fixing, if we want to know how to solve the problems of society, the solution is to strengthen our borders. If our observance of Scripture is lacking, if our morality is in disrepair, if the world is in trouble today, the solution is to increase our modesty.

There has to be a border between night and day, there has to be a border between two countries, there has to be a border between animals and humans, but the border around the bedroom has to be stronger than all of them.

The stronger our borders are, the more modest we are, the more true, the more trustworthy, the more reliable, and the more at peace we will be freeing us to pursue goodness and Godliness in a common effort, which has the makings of true peace.

As peace comes to the world, as we beat our swords into plowshares, the borders defining nations won't matter. What will matter will be the borders that define people.

Chapter 1
Have a Little Respect
for Privacy:
The Nature of Borders

Many years ago, there lived a holy man who was known to have the ability to read other people's thoughts. One day a student asked him, "Rabbi, how can you say your prayers in public around all these people with their unholy thoughts? Aren't you distracted from your prayers by knowing what's in their minds?"

The rabbi replied, "When I was a child my parents taught me not to look where I wasn't supposed to."

Why do we think that "getting close to someone" means we have to know their every private thought? We're insulted when those we love won't tell us everything. We accuse them of "hiding" from us, and we're hurt. But if you try to peek behind the curtains of someone else's privacy, you won't get any closer to that person. Quite the opposite: you'll become estranged. If a person doesn't want to reveal a part of himself or herself, then to look there is wrong.

When we are invited to become a part of someone's life, we have to be careful not to violate the other person's privacy. The respect that we have for another person's privacy—however that person has chosen to define it—enables us to nurture an intimate relationship. As soon as we trespass where we haven't been invited, we destroy the boundaries and dissipate the intimacy. In such an environment, our relationships cannot flourish.

Jewish law has great respect for privacy. If you want to build a home overlooking another home, you cannot do it in such a way that you would be able to see into your neighbor's courtyard from your window. It would be an invasion of privacy. Gossiping about others or making judgments about their behavior is also prohibited because it means you are looking into an aspect of their existence that is not open to your scrutiny. It's private, between them and God; and if you judge them, you're trespassing.

When a poor man knocks at your door and says, "I'm hungry," and your first thought is, "Why can't you get a job?", you've invaded his privacy. Why would you need to know why he can't get a job? He didn't come to discuss his inabilities or bad habits; he came to discuss his hunger. If you want to do something about it, feed him. But don't probe where you're not invited. Don't look behind the curtain he so carefully put up to protect himself.

In marriage, our most intimate relationship, respect for privacy is fundamental. A husband and wife have the right and the need for a curtain that says, "Yes, you can come into my life, for better or for worse, till death do us part, but don't peek where I don't want to be seen. Don't look at what I'm not comfortable exposing about myself. And don't expect from me what I don't want to give."

If we want to create an intimate relationship, we have to remember one simple rule of etiquette: "Be thankful for what you get, and do not expect what the other person doesn't have."

Many relationships break up not because anyone is doing anything wrong—no one is sinning, no one is cruel, no one is mean—but simply due to unfair expectations. Having unfair expectations means failing to recognize and respect another person's borders. And that constitutes an invasion of privacy.

A husband might complain about his wife: "I could understand if my wife weren't capable of meeting my expectations, if she were handicapped or paralyzed. But she can, so why doesn't she? She's so good at everything else; how can she not be good at this? If she really wanted to, I know she could, because sometimes she does."

Instead of appreciating the times that she does, those times become the poison arrows with which to shoot her: "Aha, you can! You did last month! So why don't you do it now?" He grumbles to himself, "Since she is nice sometimes, it's upsetting that she's not always nice. It would be easier if she was never nice." That's an ugly argument, and an invasion of his wife's privacy. She is comfortable being nice most of the time, but he has to go looking into those other times. Why?

Men and women do not forego the right to a private space just because they are married. We all have the right to a place where we can draw our curtain and say, "No further." Anyone who enters this space, even our spouse, is an intruder.

Where do we need more protection, more curtains, and more privacy than in our weaknesses? You can appreciate the importance of your own privacy, and your need to protect and preserve it. Your husband or wife needs that as well. To look at your spouse's weaknesses is the same as passing judgment. It's an invasion of privacy. You can't build an intimate relationship if you don't respect your spouse's borders as well as you do your own.

We are what we are, for better or worse. A wife asks, "Why isn't my husband a better person?" Ask his mother, his father, his teachers. The reply will be, "Because that's who he is."

What drives us to invade another person's privacy? Why do we need to know everything?

Maybe we're insecure. If we could know everything that was going on in every part of our spouse's personality, we would feel more secure. We don't suspect that our husbands or wives are secretly horrible people. We're not afraid of evil, just surprises. We don't want to be caught unprepared.

Or maybe our own life is so unsatisfying that we feel we have to borrow from somebody else's life. We're like the mother who must know everything her daughter says, thinks, and feels because she lives through her vicariously.

Or perhaps our motivation is a need for power. Knowing everything about the other person gives us the illusion of power. A voyeur, for example, gets a sense of power when he can see what we don't want him to see. That makes him stronger and more powerful than we are. If we can't protect our private world from his view, he's overcome us.

Some people get a real thrill out of tearing people's masks off. A wife, for example, may realize that her husband has a very strong defense mechanism. He doesn't open up and allow her to come in. By his actions, her husband is saying, "I need my curtain here; that's my defense. I cannot tolerate if you look past this curtain."

But she can't live with the fact that he won't share his most intimate thoughts, so she says, "Well, that's not healthy; I'll help you tear it down."

He protests, "I don't want to tear it down. I need you to leave it alone."

But instead of respecting his boundaries, she takes the offensive: "Those are just your facades, your defense mechanisms. I want to see who you really are."

So she tears down his curtain, and she tears down the marriage at the same time.

If we are going to preserve the intimacy of our marriage, we must recognize and respect the needs of our spouse. We should actually nurture them. Suppose you've got company over, and one of your friends brings up the one subject that is your wife's weak spot. You might say to yourself, "Good, that will force her to face the issue and tear off her mask. She needs this."

But she doesn't. Think to yourself, "They are wrong in bringing it up," but never think that your wife is wrong about her feelings. Your reaction ought to be, "Sorry, we don't talk about that here. Change the subject because it isn't a subject for our family."

Since you know that your wife has a sensitive area, a certain defense mechanism, a certain facade, a certain curtain that protects her, help her defend that curtain. You defend that curtain. Don't impose yourself on her, but be there if she needs you. Don't write off that part of her life; don't become indifferent. Be there for her, but on her terms.

If she doesn't want to go beyond a certain point, then that point becomes sacred and inviolable. Don't worry that she isn't letting her real emotions show. Leave that to the therapist.

If it's something immoral, something she shouldn't do, leave that to the clergyman. Or leave it to God. Your job is to protect her privacy for her, whatever she chooses that privacy to be.

We look at our grandparents and great-grandparents, and we wonder, why did they stay together? How could they? How did our grandmothers not see our grandfathers' glaring faults, inabilities, and handicaps? How could our grandfathers not see our grandmothers' failures and weaknesses? Most of the time, they didn't. If they noticed them at all, they looked away, because it would have been an invasion of privacy.

Today a husband might ask, "Can I just let my wife go on making her mistakes and committing sins? Is she allowed to get away with it?"

No, she's not allowed.

A husband is not responsible for his wife's morality. For this God introduced a novel idea—civil law. If a husband became responsible for his wife's morality, they would get divorced. It wouldn't be an intimate relationship; it wouldn't be even a friendship.

To preserve friendship and intimacy, you respect the other person's privacy. You don't look at his or her faults. If you accidentally trip over them, you look away.

Many years ago, in a small village in Europe, a woman committed adultery. She was very worried, because she had heard that if you commit adultery, you're not allowed to stay married to your husband and you're not allowed to marry the person with whom you committed adultery. She went to the rabbi and said, "Rabbi, what should I do? I committed adultery."

The rabbi answered, "I have to think about it. Come back tomorrow."

The next day, she returned. She said, "So, Rabbi, what do you think?"

"About what?"

"About what I told you yesterday."

The rabbi said, "I'm sorry, I don't remember." She repeated her story, and he told her to return again the next day. She kept telling her story; he kept forgetting.

The moral is that even a rabbi has to sometimes behave like a husband. When the woman said that she committed adultery, he either didn't hear, or forgot, or dismissed it. He looked away.

Husbands and wives, however, should never try to play rabbi to one another. You can't confuse the two. Yes, there are moral obligations. But are you her rabbi or are you her husband? Are you his mentor or are you his wife? If you can help the other spouse not sin and not do what is wrong, that's wonderful. You'll grow together. But that's not your main responsibility.

The fact that your spouse isn't perfect shouldn't be your problem. If your husband or wife were perfect, then you wouldn't need any talent or wisdom. The idea is that this person isn't perfect, and it doesn't bother you. It's not your problem because you accept your spouse unconditionally.

We are not talking about dangerous misbehavior or physical violence, just normal, human imperfections. You don't have to just tolerate your spouse. When your husband or wife continually rubs you the wrong way, eventually that friction will start a fire. So it's not enough simply to tolerate your spouse's faults. You have to be like the sons of Noah and not see them.

The Bible tells us that one day, one of Noah's sons entered the tent where Noah was sleeping, and saw that his father was naked. When he came out, he told the other brothers.

The other two brothers entered the tent, covered their father, "and their father's nakedness they did not see" (Gen. 9:22–23). They saw that he needed to be covered. If someone is uncovered, you simply go and cover him. You see what needs to be done, but you don't look for faults. You might see the condition, but you don't judge the person. Noah's sons didn't see a nakedness in their father.

If there is something your husband or wife doesn't want you to notice, you don't look. You don't think, "I see my spouse's faults, but I'll bite my tongue and not say anything." That's not going to last long, and you'll end up with a bloody tongue.

The happier thought is, "I know my spouse isn't perfect, but I don't notice anything wrong. I'm not being a martyr, I'm not putting up with anything, I'm not long-suffering. I like what he or she is."

The reason you don't notice is not because you're so kind, so wise, and so magnanimous that you overlook your spouse's faults. It's not overlooking; it's having respect for your mate's privacy.

That's how so many great-grandparents could find contentment with each other. They looked where they were supposed to, at what they were invited to see, and not where they weren't invited.

So, in your marriage, appreciate what is there and, don't worry so much about what isn't. Don't focus on the differences but on the things you agree upon. If you don't notice her faults, you'll love her for what she is. If you don't notice where his opinions aren't your opinions, you love him for his inner self.

You're not waiting, you're not counting, you're not keeping score.

You're not being a martyr; you're simply being decent.

You're not settling for less; you're getting more.

You're not being noble; you're simply respecting borders.

Chapter 2
Who Deserves Better?
Remembering Our
Purpose

When I was a child, a wise, older man used to visit my school and decided to look in on the classroom where we were studying. Peeking over one of our shoulders, he noticed that we happened to be learning the idea of self-evaluation.

He was a warm and humorous man, and he said, "You know, when Yom Kippur, the Day of Atonement, comes around, you have to make an account of yourself, so you do a lot of soul-searching. But what is that? How do you do it?"

He waited, but we were too timid to reply. So he smiled and said, "Well, I'll tell you what it isn't. Imagine today is Yom Kippur, the Day of Atonement. It's been ten days since Rosh Hoshana, the Jewish New Year, ten days known as the Days of Repentance. Our thoughts have been getting holier and holier, more serious with each passing day, as we've tried to become better.

"Finally, Yom Kippur has arrived. We put on white garments, we dress like angels, we think like angels, we act like angels. We don't eat, we don't drink, we don't sleep. We don't wear leather shoes. It's Yom Kippur, the holiest day of the year.

"Everybody gets together in the holiest place in town, in the synagogue. Then, together, as a community, we spend the entire day thinking about sins. We think about what sins we committed last January, what sins we committed last February, last March, and on and on. We do this because we want to make an account, search our souls. We want to ask the Master of the Universe to forgive any sins we might have committed against Him throughout the entire year.

"So we dredge them up. We think hard to remember every sin we committed in the course of this year. Here we are, the entire community, sitting around on the holiest day of the year, in the holiest place in town, wallowing in unholy memories! And by doing this we are supposed to become holy? This is how we are going to become refined? This is how we are supposed to make things better?

"That is certainly not soul-searching. That's degrading. It's not nice any day of the year, and certainly not on the Day of Atonement. What, then, does it mean to regret our sins?

"Not by dredging up sins, not by spending the holiest day of the year thinking about unholy, sinful memories. Proper soul-searching, true soul-searching, has nothing to do with sins, nothing to do with misdeeds, nothing to do with ugly memories. It has to do with a relationship.

"What it means to take stock of yourself and do an account of your soul, to search your soul, is to consider where your relationship stands. It does not mean to consider the sins you have committed. If you have sinned, then the sin is that you have violated your relationship with your God.

"What you should dwell on, what you should contemplate, what you should force yourself to think about, is this: Who is your God, how great He is, and how good He has been to you. Then, how could you mistreat Him? How could you have forgotten Him in the course of a year?

"Serving God is the purpose for which you were created. How could you have neglected His teachings, how could you have overlooked them, how could you have been careless about them?

"Think about how much you need Him, how much He does for you, how good He's been to you in the past year, how great He is in general, how true He is, and how holy He is.

"When you stop to reflect on this for even a moment—not a full day, but for one moment—you realize it is this God to whom you have been careless and lax in your devotion. It immediately hurts. You feel an intense stab of regret. How could you?

"How could you forget the purpose for which you were created? How could you be that way to such a God, to your God? And that is true repentance. Then you have truly taken an account of yourself, truly searched your soul, in the context of your relationship with God. Then you have begun to make things better."

The lessons of this story also hold true in marriage. Are you trying to be a perfect wife because you are so hung-up on being perfect? Are you a nice husband because you want to think of yourself as a nice person, or because your wife deserves it?

Have you spent time thinking about the person to whom you are married? Do you believe that caring for this one person really is the purpose for which you were created when God planned the world?

If you concentrate on what your spouse means to you, how important and necessary the relationship is, then it becomes easier to be a little better—because your spouse deserves it. The man who's determined to be a good husband "whether his wife likes it or not," who's determined to be a model husband, is not a real husband. Why is he so determined to be a good husband? Because he likes to excel at what he does? Because when he was a child, he was in the habit of getting A's?

This misunderstanding happens all the time in religion. Why should we be good? Because we like being good? Or because we are fulfilling the purpose for which we were created, to serve

God? There are people who observe all of God's commandments, even going beyond the letter of the law, with the attitude, "I'm going to do this whether God likes it or not." They're not coming to religion out of acceptance of God, but in response to a need they have, like the husband who is determined to be perfect whether his wife likes it or not.

These people may need to have law and order in their lives, they may need to have a focus in their lives, they may need to have a goal, or a structure, or virtue. They may need to get to heaven. And their attitude is that they are going to get to heaven whether God likes it or not. They believe observing God's commandments is not a matter of doing what God wants; it's doing what they want, which is to keep the commandments. The focus of their life is on the commandments, rather than on responding to the Giver of those commandments.

A rather scholarly young seminary student once said as much to me. He told me, "You know, I don't believe in faith." So I asked him, "How can you call yourself a devoted Jew? To be a devoted Jew means you accept with an absolute faith that God gave us the commandments to live by."

His answer was, "Well, concerning the giving of the commandments, I acknowledge the need to have faith. But other than the actual commandments, I don't believe in faith. I accept on faith that God tells me to observe the commandments as they are recorded in Scripture. But if God were to tell me to do anything else, that I couldn't accept on faith."

So I said to him, "Never mind the question, how can anything God says not be considered a divine commandment? But could you explain to me why you think you need to accept the commandments in the Scripture on faith? Why do you have faith in that situation, but not in any other?"

His response was, "Because it says to in the Bible, and I believe in the Bible." He was saying, in effect, "The Bible says to accept God; therefore I do, because I accept the Bible." His reasoning was completely inverted.

Whose Bible was he accepting? God's Bible. He was saying he believed in God because God's Bible tells him to, but not the other way around, not, "I accept the Bible because God tells me to." The object of his acceptance was the Bible but not the Giver of the Bible.

And, of course, the same can be true in a marriage. The emphasis should be on your spouse, not on yourself. In a relationship, you may forget to think about yourself, but never the other person.

We know this from a prayer recited on Yom Kippur, the Day of Atonement, in which we ask forgiveness for those sins we committed with "confusion of the heart." The sins we committed with "confusion of the heart" means the sins we committed in panic. Now why would we have to ask forgiveness for such sins? How can it be a sin to be panicked?

Imagine that you are on a sinking ship. Everyone panics. You flee for your life. If you forget to worry about one of your friends, he might be disappointed but it would be understandable. "Every man for himself" isn't considered a sin.

But if you forget your wife, if you panic and jump into the lifeboat without her, leaving her to fend for herself, nobody will forgive you. That would be considered a sin.

You might say, "I panicked," but panic can only reach so far. Panic is not an excuse if a husband or wife bails out of a sinking ship and forgets the other, because that kind of relationship is too deep for panic.

Some people seem to be generally lax and careless about their relationships, but in a state of emergency they rise to the occasion and become heroes. In spite of the panic they may be feeling, their commitment to their relationships suddenly becomes sharply defined. That's because those things deep within the soul cannot be affected by panic.

In the context of our relationship with God, we are not supposed to panic. We have to ask forgiveness for the very fact that we allowed panic to reach us more deeply than the relationship. Even when we are panicked, we are not supposed to forget who God is.

In the context of your relationship with your spouse, you are not allowed to forget for a moment to whom you are married, to whom you are devoted. If you really want to make things better, you need to stop thinking about yourself. Stop thinking in terms of being a husband or wife; stop thinking about what you are.

People are always looking for ways to "improve their relationships." But the first question to ask is, "What is the morality of this relationship?" Are you in it for yourself, or are you in it for your spouse? Find out first where your heart lies, and where your devotion is. Is it to yourself? If so, that's immoral. Or is it to your spouse?

It could be that the relationship needs to improve. Maybe intimacy is lacking. But ask yourself what your motivation is. Why do you want to improve it? Why do you want to make things better? If your answer is, "Well, I just can't stand that person any longer," or, "I deserve better," then your motivation is not what it ought to be.

Maybe you think that you deserve a better life. After all, when you were younger, you had your first job, and you liked it for a while. Then you began to feel a little bit out of place because you thought you "deserved" better. A better job with better perks. You drove a certain car for a while, until you felt that maybe you "deserved" a bigger car, a better car. Could the same be true of your marriage? All of a sudden, you've decided that you "deserve" better. You are older, wiser, and better, but your spouse hasn't gotten any better. No problem, just trade in the old one for a newer model.

Or maybe you tell yourself, "Look, there are certain things I get from my wife. That's fine. I'm married to her and I want to stay married to her. I don't have any intention of breaking up our family, God forbid! I have no thoughts of a divorce! But you know, you can't get everything from one woman. So for what I don't get from my wife, well, there's always the secretary. But the secretary isn't competing with my wife. My wife is my wife. My wife is my marriage. We're a family. It's just for those things that I can't get from her that I go somewhere else."

Nobody is going to buy that kind of thinking. Why? What's wrong with it?

It's true you can't get everything you want from one person, but then, who says you need everything? Where did you get the idea you deserve everything?

The issue is not what you deserve. The issue is, whom are you here to serve? Yourself, or your spouse? Yourself, or God?

Do you deserve what you already have? The answer is yes. The answer is always yes, because God is just, and God is right. You have exactly what you deserve, exactly what you need. In learning to accept your spouse, to accept your life, to accept the purpose for which you were created, you need to feel grateful and accept graciously what you have. What you need, God provides. What you can't get, or what you don't have, you probably don't need. You may think you do, but you don't.

A woman who thought she needed her husband to be more romantic once spoke to me. She said, "He's responsible, he's kind, he's good, but he has no romance in him. He goes to work, he comes home, and every week he brings home a paycheck. But our life together seems so dry and mechanical. He's making me crazy because he's so unromantic."

Anyone who knew this woman knew she could have been a drill sergeant. So I said to her, "What are you talking about? If your husband suddenly became romantic on you, you'd send him to a psychiatrist."

"Why do you say that?" she asked. I told her, "Because you're not at all the romantic type yourself. You're a very practical, down-to-earth pragmatic person. Everything about you is efficient. It may seem cliche, but what's bothering you is a case of 'the grass is greener' way of thinking.

"You're only kidding yourself, because in reality, you'd hate it if he turned 'romantic' on you. You'd think he's being foolish, childish, and irresponsible.

"You've been married to him for seven years in spite of the fact that he isn't romantic. But if he weren't reliable and responsible, you wouldn't have stayed married to him for a month. Think about it."

She laughed and agreed with me. She admitted that what she values most in other people is their organization and efficiency, that what she appreciates most is their ability to "get things done."

She was confusing romance with intimacy. As long as her husband was being sensitive to what she really needed, and eventually she realized that he was, her marriage was in good shape.

If you think that you're unhappy or unsatisfied because you "need" something, think again. Having a relationship that lasts forever means trusting that it will provide everything you need, and realizing that the things it can't provide, you probably don't need. The things you do need are there if you look deeply enough.

What you really need is to believe that you are married to the person you are meant to be married to.

God wants His children to be happy. He entrusted this one person to your care because He wants you to make this person happy. That is your purpose in life. It's not a question of how good a wife you can be. It's not a question of what you are.

What you should look for, what should motivate you, why you should want your relationship to become better and more intimate, is, "Because my spouse deserves it. My spouse deserves better."

Why are you in this relationship? Because you were young and restless, so you got married? Because your mother talked you into it? No. Because you were created for it. This was an essential part of God's plan. There is one person whom you're supposed to make happy, there is one God whom you have to serve, there is one Scripture that you have to study, and that's your purpose in life.

It will never get better if your attitude is, "You do for me, then I'll do for you." What matters is, are you devoted to each other? Are you friends? Are you in this together? Do you care about one another? When the answer is "yes," then you can begin to think about making a better life together. Then you are free to think in terms that say you accept this other person as being your purpose in life.

Without this, our sages tell us, "You would be better off not having been born." Because if you're not going to fulfill the purpose for which you were created, then you don't really exist. You were created for a purpose, and that purpose justifies your existence.

So if you want to make a better life together, think about what is right and good and wonderful about the other person. If that becomes your focus, then the thought that you were once not nice or careless or insensitive immediately feels very uncomfortable. You will regret it intensely, and you will become nicer, more careful, and more sensitive.

And your life will be better, together.

Chapter 3
Taking Someone Else Seriously: Becoming One Flesh

It says in the Bible, "Therefore shall a man leave his father and mother, and cleave to his wife, and become one flesh" (Gen. 2:24). What does this mean, "one flesh"?

It could simply mean the body of the child born to a father and mother since, in the conception and birth of a child, man and woman "become one flesh." But then why didn't God just say, "Get together and have children"?

Because what God was talking about was more than physical. Such merging is impossible in the physical world. But husband and wife are more than physical, and marriage is intended to be a divine institution. On a spiritual level, therefore, husband and wife are capable of a unique and wondrous unity. And on that level, "becoming one" refers to intimacy.

Yet if God was trying to tell Adam and Eve that He intended marriage to be intimate, why didn't He say, "Become one heart, one mind, and one soul"? Because becoming one flesh refers to an intimacy even greater than that of being of one heart, one mind, and one soul.

As far as souls are concerned, husband and wife are already two halves of the same soul, reunited at the time of marriage. They don't need to become one because they are one, and have always been since the time of creation.

As far as minds are concerned, to "become of one mind" is not unique to marriage. Friends can be of one mind.

To be of a single heart is also not unique to marriage. When the Children of Israel stood together at Mt. Sinai to receive the commandments, they were gathered there with a single purpose, "like one person with one heart" (Commentary of Rashi on Exod. 19:2).

Being of one flesh is more intimate than being of one soul, one mind, and one heart, because marriage accomplishes what no other relationship can accomplish: man and woman becoming one in the concerns of the flesh.

To fully comprehend the idea of one flesh, we first need to understand the concept of two types of souls. The human being functions on two levels: the immortal godly level, and the mortal natural level.

The immortal soul, which is of God, refers to that part of our personality in which we experience godly feelings and yearnings to be like God, to imitate God's ways even in the physical world. The mortal soul is that part of our personality that can relate to purely earthly needs. When we talk about the concerns of the flesh, we are referring to that state of mind, those characteristics, feelings, and emotions that come from the physical body in which we exist. By sharing the concerns of the flesh, that is, the needs of their mortal souls, husband and wife become one.

When we talk about the needs of the mortal soul, we mean more than physical needs such as eating, sleeping, and reproducing. We also mean the needs of the ego: the need to defend ourselves against insult, the need for recognition, the need to feel significant, the need to be respected, the need to be appreciated, the need to be understood, the need to be secure. All of these are the needs of our human condition: our mortal soul.

We recognize these needs in our children. Every child needs to be nurtured, protected, made to feel secure, defended against insult, recognized, understood, and appreciated. Yet the mature person, the person of virtue, is someone who has managed to transcend these needs, who can overlook an insult, who doesn't need to defend himself constantly, and who would rather give than receive respect.

In our efforts to be more godly, our goal as we mature is to grow away from the needs of the mortal soul toward the needs of the immortal soul. By giving us commandments to follow, God let us know that we can transcend the needs of the body, and likewise the needs of our mortal soul.

There is nothing sacred or absolute about the demands of the mortal soul. For example, although the body needs to eat, God commanded the Jews to fast on Yom Kippur, the Day of Atonement. No one is horrified by the thought of fasting on that occasion.

The same is true with almost every physical need the body has. There are times when we say "no," and times when we are told to say "no." Either way, the message is clear that the needs of the body, of the physical condition, are not absolute.

A fifteen-year-old rabbinic student was once staying for a time in his teacher's home. The teacher, taking the obligation of hospitality seriously, would allow no one to serve the boy but himself. On the first morning, when the student came down for breakfast, the older man said, "Here, have a little of this, and a little more of that. Take more! This is fresh, and this is good," and so forth. The boy ate everything that was placed in front of him.

That evening, walking home from the synagogue together, the teacher said to the boy, "I hope you don't mind my saying this, but a person can't be like an animal, eating food just because it's in front of him. You don't have to eat everything you see. You can control yourself."

"I don't understand. You told me to eat it."

"Yes, I told you to eat it, but who says you had to eat?"

The student thought, "Okay, okay, I get the message." But the next morning, the teacher said to the student, "Here, have a little of this, and a little more of this. And try this; it's homemade."

Walking home that night, he again scolded the boy. "You really need to control your appetite. You can't indulge yourself in everything you want."

After this happened a number of times, the boy said to the older man, "What do you want from me? You're driving me crazy! First you tell me to eat, then you tell me not to eat. Tell me what you want!"

"What do I want? I don't want anything. In the morning, you are my guest. As a host, I can't tell you to control your appetite, not while you are sitting at the table in my kitchen. Then it's my obligation to serve you, which I do.

"But it's not your obligation to eat so much. So, as your teacher, it's my responsibility to train you, and share with you some of my learning."

Ideally, becoming an adult means understanding that we don't need to gratify our every desire, and that it isn't necessary to defend our egos at all costs. We are then more likely to be able to care for someone else's needs, and to defend someone else's ego.

"Now," you might say, "wait a minute. I just finished growing up and it took me twenty years to learn that my ego is not sacred. Now you're telling me that I should take someone else's ego seriously. It seems like going backwards."

It's not going backwards at all. It's a giant step forward. You have felt the need to be appreciated, to be respected, to feel secure; but after twenty years of growth and maturity, you've come to realize that you don't absolutely have to be appreciated or respected or feel secure. Your ego does not at all times have to be gratified.

To yourself, become the boy's teacher, saying, "I don't really need this, and I don't have to have that." Admonish yourself, never others, unless it is your place to teach. Instead, you should treat others as the host treated the boy.

Once you have discovered your own earthy needs and impulses, your ego's desire to be recognized, and the wants of your mortal soul, you are capable of gratifying those very needs in someone else. To those around you, you should say, "Here, this is for you, and this is for you. Let me do this for you, and let me get that for you."

I had a great-uncle who was a wonderful example to me. He was a humble man. The events of his life had humbled him—he had lived through the war, his wife had died at a young age, and he had no children; but he was also humble through personal virtue. He lived alone, and from time to time he came to our house for dinner. He was very gentle, rarely spoke, and never raised his voice. Because we were young, we thought him a little senile.

One day we were sitting at the kitchen table. My mother was standing at the sink, and I asked her to hand me a spoon. This gentle old man turned livid; he became indignant and quite beside himself.

He said, "*Banutzin zich mit di mamen?*" In other words, why are you using your mother? Sending her on an errand for you?

That was all. Then he was silent once more.

Why was he livid with indignation? He was morally outraged that a child could say to a mother, "Get me this, get me that." A child should get up and get it for himself. Sending a mother was unheard of and unthinkable.

This was a man who never asked for anything. He never asked us to carry packages for him, to come to his apartment, to move furniture, never a request for himself. To his mind, who was he to ask a favor of someone else?

But my mother's honor was a different matter. On someone else's behalf, the man who never spoke for himself would speak out. What he had learned to dismiss in himself he took very seriously in others. Life had taught him its lessons well. (Incidentally, my mother never noticed my indiscretion.)

This is what distinguishes us from the children we once were. Having gotten bigger than our own egos, we can now take someone else's ego seriously. The next step, the logical step, the godly step, is to appreciate someone else, to respect someone else, to make someone else feel secure. And for this we are now qualified.

That's why we wait to be married until we are ready to be married, when we are grown, and able take on the responsibility for another person's mortal soul—having finally mastered our own.

Then we remind ourselves, "The needs of my mortal soul are there so I can understand what another person is feeling, and take care of that person's needs; to take care of my own would be hedonistic. Now that I have felt the need for respect, for appreciation, and for security, I know how to respect, appreciate, and make someone else feel secure."

When we deny the needs of our mortal soul, yet gratify those same needs in someone else, we imitate God. Then we are free to proceed along the lines of spiritual growth. Then we think, feel, and act in a holy manner, in a way that is like God. Just as God is merciful to us, we learn to be merciful to others. Just as God forgives us, we learn to forgive others, and so on.

Where do we really see all of this practiced? In marriage. When does all this really get put into effect? In marriage.

Marriage is the arena in which all we discover on the way to becoming "like God" is put into practice. To be devoted to a relationship means to be devoted to the other person's needs, more so than to your own. It means taking on the other person's needs as though they were yours. In so doing, two people merge into one.

This same oneness occurs in the metaphysical realm. In trying to grasp a godly subject, for example, the mind simultaneously envelops the subject and is itself surrounded by the subject. This double oneness or mutual merging, where each object both surrounds and is surrounded by the other, is a divine occurrence. When husband and wife become one flesh, they bridge the gap between what is physical and what is spiritual, between what is mortal and what is immortal, between what is merely human and what is godly. And they do this on a daily basis, in a way that only two people who are married can do.

In that way, husband and wife are truly capable of a unique and wondrous unity, a double oneness.

Chapter 4
What Does
"Happily Ever After"
Really Mean?
The Sanctity of Marriage

One day, when I was walking down the street with one of my teachers, we were approached by a young couple. The wife said to my teacher, "Isn't it true that stirring the soup while it's on the stove would violate the Sabbath? Tell my husband—he doesn't know!"

My teacher looked thoughtful for a minute and said, "I'll have to look it up and get back to you." The couple went on.

Then, noticing my puzzled expression, my teacher explained, "You're surprised at my answer because the wife's question was such a simple one. You and I both know that she was correct. But for me to have known the answer without so much as a glance at 'The Code of Jewish Law' would have made her husband appear foolish."

My teacher had wisely chosen to allow himself to appear foolish, rather than diminish a husband in his wife's eyes. Why? Because marriage is sacred. To do anything that diminishes it, discourages it, or dulls it is wrong. To say something discouraging or disparaging about a husband to a wife, about a wife to a husband, is an unpardonable sin.

Marriage is a holy institution, as holy as a congregation at prayer. Because of this, husband and wife are capable of a unique and wondrous unity.

If we walk into a room where people are praying, we acknowledge that something holy is taking place. We wait in reverence, careful not to distract them from their prayers. We should feel a similar reverence in the presence of a husband and wife. Acknowledging the sanctity of marriage, we should be careful not to distract them from each other, or in any way dampen their enthusiasm for each other.

One of the more serious sins—on a par with idol worship and blasphemy—is the sin of discouraging another person from his or her relationship with God (Deut. 13:7-19; Talmud, Ethics of the Fathers 5:18). One who attempts to dampen another's enthusiasm for God is deserving of the worst punishment. We're not supposed to have compassion for this person, or go out of our way to find extenuating circumstances, as we would do in the case of any other sin.

Likewise, we're not allowed to disparage other people before God, even while disparaging ourselves. One of the prophets, in an attempt to humble himself before God, said, "How can I be worthy of prophecy when I am unclean of lips, and I live among a people who are unclean of lips," a reference to his fellow Jews. God chastised him, saying, "You may call yourself unclean, but don't you dare say that about My children" (Isa. 6:5-7).

This is because our relationship with God is like a marriage. To come to a wife and say derogatory things about her husband is unconscionable; by the same token, to come to the husband and say nasty things about his wife is intolerable. But, unknowingly, we often find ourselves doing just that.

At a party or family gathering, for example, we may be so charming and witty that everyone else pales by comparison. In this way, although it is unintentional, we may make a husband look bad in the presence of his wife, or make a wife look bad in the presence of her husband. We must be aware of this possibility.

One of the holiest acts is to bring peace between a husband and wife. This doesn't mean that if the husband and wife are fighting, we ought to referee the fight. That would bring a cease-fire, but it wouldn't bring peace.

Bringing peace to a husband and wife means that on every occasion, whenever we have the chance, we should enhance the husband's opinion of his wife and the wife's opinion of her husband. Help the husband appreciate his wife, and the wife respect her husband—before there's a problem, as my teacher did. That helps to prevent the problem. That's what is meant by promoting peace, not a cease-fire between husband and wife.

Since marriage is a holy institution, that holiness has to be treated with the respect it deserves. The way to do that is by helping one appreciate the other, certainly not by criticizing one to the other.

How should you react when someone criticizes your spouse? You're not supposed to be objective. We used to hear people say, "Well, what do you expect? She's his wife, so he'll never see anything wrong with her." That's the way you're supposed to be.

A wife shouldn't have to be superwoman for her husband to feel loyal to her, and a husband shouldn't have to be superman for his wife to feel loyal to him. Loyalty comes from the fact that you realize that this other person is so central to your life that it is this relationship that gives your life meaning.

When you find yourselves on opposite sides of the fence because one of you made a mistake, that's disloyalty. It's like getting divorced. Suddenly, you aren't married anymore; you're wishing you were outside the marriage. This often occurs in ways that are subtle, but real and serious.

For example, before getting married, he brings her home for his mother's approval, which is as it should be. But long after they're married, he still needs his mother to approve of his wife.

Every time they go to his parents' house, although they arrive as a couple, he soon becomes his mother's son. His wife gets the feeling that she has once again become a stranger to him. This is especially true if his mother is actually critical of his wife.

Against your spouse, the outsider is never right. If your husband's boss is telling him that he's no good, then the boss is wrong. Always. Against anybody else, whether it's at home or outside the home, you have to be loyal to your spouse.

But too often, that isn't the case. A man goes out to work but tells his wife not to call him because it bothers him. Is that being loyal? Is that being the man in her life? No, that's being the man in her evenings—if he gets home from work before she goes to bed. When he does go out with her, if she doesn't look the way he wants her to look, he pretends he doesn't know her. He spends his time talking to other people, and forgets that he's with her.

While they're at a party, he knocks over the drinks, messing up the tablecloth and himself. His wife makes a face, turns to the person next to her, and says, "He's such a klutz." The person sitting next to her is a stranger; the person with the wet shirt is her husband. Yet she turns from him to this stranger, and says, "He's such a klutz." She has cut herself off from him emotionally, severed her relationship, and—for the moment—divorced herself from him.

Then the two of them go to a marriage counselor, and the husband says, "Can you figure her out?" He's saying to the therapist, "You and I—we're smart; we're okay. Let's figure her out." He's not on her side; he wants to be on the therapist's side. It's easy to understand why the two of them are having problems. Because he doesn't identify with her, and she doesn't identify with him.

Once a child was sitting at the window, looking out wistfully. His father passed by and said, "You know, if you're going to be wistful, it's better to be on the outside looking in than on the inside looking out."

That's the way we ought to feel about our marriages. Given a choice, it's better to be unmarried but thinking, "I wish I was," than to be inside a marriage feeling like an outsider. All too often, people who are married to one another feel like outsiders. At the slightest provocation, and for the silliest reason, they step out of the relationship. It's a terrible thing to do, but we all do it, and for the silliest reasons.

For example, a husband and wife go shopping and arrive at the cash register with their purchases. The clerk, whom they don't know, says, "That'll be seventeen dollars." The wife then takes out a ten dollar bill and puts it down. The clerk repeats, "It's seventeen dollars." The wife says, "Oh, I'm sorry, I thought you said seven." Then the husband looks at the clerk, shakes his head in exasperation, and says, "She does this all the time."

As soon as something feels slightly uncomfortable, the husband backs out of his relationship with his wife, as if she's the stranger. He sides with anyone who happens to be there, even if it's just the clerk behind the counter. This is someone he never met before and might never see again, yet he wants to be on the clerk's side, against his wife. That's disloyalty; that's stepping out of the relationship.

A carload of seminary students was driving from New York to Boston to attend a wedding when their car was struck by a truck. The gas tank ignited and the station wagon, with the nine boys in it, went up in flames. Miraculously, they were left with nothing worse than a few scars. When their teacher in New York learned of the accident, and of the boys' survival, he reported the news to the dean of the seminary.

The dean asked, "Who gave them permission to go?" Without batting an eyelash, the teacher said, "I did."

It wasn't true. He had not given them permission. He had, in fact, told them not to go. But his devotion and commitment to his students was such that he instinctively defended them, even though it meant being chastised himself. That's being loyal; that's being inside a relationship.

You need that kind of reflex in marriage. Once you come out from under that marriage canopy, the world should be forever different. Never again can you take an outsider's perspective.

The fairy tales and storybooks that begin, "Once upon a time," always end, "and they lived happily ever after." Why did they live happily ever after? Didn't they have arguments? Didn't they have bills to pay? Didn't they have uncooperative children? Of course they did. But "once upon a time" they were loyal to each other.

"Happily ever after" means that two people find wholeness in each other. The loyalty they feel for one another comes from the fact that, primarily, they exist for each other.

According to Jewish mysticism, Adam and Eve were once one person. God divided them, and turned each half into a separate person. Therefore a man goes searching for a wife, and a woman goes searching for a husband. If we lose something we once had, we search for it.

Alone, each one of us feels like only half a being. That's why we are so uncomfortable being alone. The feeling of halfness begins as soon as a child is born, when the umbilical cord is severed. As long as a child is attached to the cord, its mother is the other half.

When adolescents begin to separate from their parents, the sensation of halfness becomes intense. Adolescent infatuations don't come from a need to be popular, but from a more basic need: a need to feel whole. Being half is so unpleasant that any promise of wholeness, any interest from another "half," is irresistible—sometimes more irresistible than an adolescent can handle.

Each of us needs to experience the pain of halfness in order to get married. Without feeling our own halfness, we aren't able to let someone else into our lives. We need to feel that we really are half and not whole; and that by remaining alone, we'll never be whole.

Experiencing our own halfness, tasting it and admitting it, prepares us for marriage. When we are married to another person, we no longer feel like a half; without marriage, the feeling of halfness would be intolerable for most people.

Mrs. Anatoly Shcharansky traveled around the world for nine years trying to secure the release of her husband from a Russian prison. During all that time, she was Mrs. Shcharansky.

You could say, "He was arrested right after the wedding. All they had was a ceremony. They didn't even get to know each other as husband and wife. Was there ever a Mrs. Shcharansky? There may have been a wedding, but there really wasn't much of a marriage. So nine years later, why is she still calling herself Mrs. Shcharansky?

What made her so devoted to this man in Russia? Just because, nine years earlier, they stood before an official who performed their wedding ceremony?"

She was devoted because he was her husband, she was his wife, and their marriage was sacred. She was loyal to him because nine years earlier, she ceased being half a being; she was a whole being, and her other half, her husband, was now in jail.

So what does "happily ever after" really mean? It means that you never step out of the relationship and look into the marriage, at your wife or your husband, like an outsider. It means that you accept that this person is your purpose in life, and that it's a sacred responsibility to make him or her happy. If your husband or wife happens to have a problem, and you have to take care of that problem, that's not an interference in your life. That is your life. He is your life. She is your life.

If the two of you wholeheartedly believe that this is what your lives are all about, and acknowledge the sanctity of your marriage, the result will be loyalty and reverence to one another. That doesn't mean there won't be problems. But when a marriage accomplishes what it's supposed to accomplish, the half becomes a sacred whole. A sacred whole, a unique and wondrous unity, can take care of problems. That's when it's "happily ever after."

Chapter 5
So You Want to Be
a Nice Person?
Loyalty, Respect, and
Devotion in Action

Many years ago, a woman had a very serious problem. She was twenty-six years old, and as lonely as a stone in a field. She didn't have a single friend, couldn't get along with anyone, and couldn't keep a relationship. Why? Because, to put it bluntly, her behavior was obnoxious.

She was petty, she was selfish, she was jealous, and she was cruel. She tried desperately to control her negative traits, and spent years in every kind of counseling and therapy, without success. When she thought she had reached the end of her rope, she heard that there was a wise, saintly man in Brooklyn who might be able to help her with her problem, Rabbi Menachem M. Schneerson, leader of the worldwide Lubavitch movement. She came to him and presented him with an eight-page analysis of her problem.

The venerable rabbi, known as the "Rebbe," gave her some very simple advice. He told her that when she returned to the college campus where she was attending school, she should make it a habit to serve other people during meals.

"Whatever it is that someone else might need," the Rebbe said, "the butter, the sugar, the salt, a glass of water, whatever it is, it should become your habit to bring it to them." The woman was relieved. Instead of analyzing her, the Rebbe had given her something she could actually do.

Looking back, she saw it this way: "A selfish, petty, egotistical person came to the Rebbe, and said, 'Rebbe, I need advice. I don't know what to do. I'm not a nice person. What should I do?'

"And the Rebbe said, in effect, 'Not nice? So be nice. What's the question? You don't like being not nice? So, who's forcing you? You want to be nice? Good. Then here's how you start: Bring somebody a glass of water.' " In other words, if you're not a nice person, don't stop and analyze it. Just start thinking, speaking, and acting in a nice manner.

The same is true with love, respect, appreciation, or any of the emotions necessary in a relationship. Everyone has a capacity for love, respect, and appreciation. You know when you need it, you know when you want it, and you know when you're not getting it.

It has been written that one kind thought, one holy word, and one good deed can change the world. The area in which this is most important is in marriage. That's where what you think, what you say, and how you act can really make a difference.

For example, one woman coming to a marriage counselor might say, "My husband's heart is in the right place, and I know he means well, but he acts just terribly. I know he really loves me, but he speaks to me abusively, he criticizes me all the time, and he mistreats me in front of other people."

Another woman might say, "My husband is a very nice man. He's responsible, he speaks very nicely, he's thoughtful and considerate, but I'm not sure if he loves me in his heart of hearts, from the depths of his soul."

We would understand if the first woman wanted a divorce. But the second woman would be out of her mind to ask for a divorce. If her husband thinks lovingly, speaks lovingly, and acts lovingly, what more could she ask? She has a good marriage. She should leave his "heart of hearts" and the "depths of his soul" alone, and go home and be happy that she's married to a nice man.

The same is true when you talk about yourself. The answer to your problems doesn't always lie in analyzing your inner workings, or in probing the depths of your soul to find out why you feel the way you feel. The important thing is, how do you act?

Are you a nice person? If not, what are you going to do about it? Why analyze it? Do you need to know why, or do you need to start being nice? If you want to be nice, start today. Think nice thoughts, speak nice words, do something nice for someone. In the end, you will in fact be nice.

Sometimes it's better not to start probing the workings of your soul. Those are complicated streets in there, and you might not know your way around. It's easy to get lost, and you haven't even got a map. So stick to what you do know. You know how to think, you know how to speak, and you know how to act. That's something you have control over.

People who go through years of therapy spend too much time completely occupied with themselves. It would be better for them to stop relying on therapy, and just do something good for a change.

So how can we bring love, respect, and devotion to our relationships? It's easy. You already know how deeply you need to be loved and how profoundly you want to be recognized. Now take that information and apply it to your relationships. You know what love really means, so love someone else. You know how important gratitude is, so show a little gratitude.

And you know how much you need respect, so be a little more respectful.

A respectful person is someone who has a talent for respect, a knack for it, a skill. A respectful person is not someone who can respect only geniuses, saints, or prophets. He or she has the capacity to respect everybody.

The same is true of a loving person. A loving person doesn't love only the person who saved his life on the beach. Anyone can do that. A loving person is someone who can love without being caused to love. Such love doesn't have to be earned; he or she offers it willingly.

A loving person can love the poor soul whom everyone else rejects and ignores. Why do other people ignore an unlovable creature? They're waiting for him to earn their love. But if he's a real loser, he can't. The loving person doesn't wait. He doesn't react; he initiates. He has a capacity to love.

Is love something you want for yourself, or something you give to others? Do you have only the capacity to receive, or can you give as well?

Think about your capacity for compassion. Suppose a poor woman knocks on your door and says, "Could I please have something to eat?" You look at her, and think, "She doesn't look that emaciated." So you tell her, "Sorry, come back when you're skinnier. When you move me to compassion." That's not compassion. Compassion isn't something that has to be forced on you. Where is your ability to feel compassion? If it has to be forced on you, it isn't real.

What about your marriage? When your husband or wife needs a little respect, do you give it? Sure, you'll give it—when your spouse is perfect, then you'll respect him or her? No, you won't, because with those conditions, you're not capable of respect.

The question is, will you respect your spouse, or won't you? It's not what your spouse does or doesn't do; it's you. Where is your respect? Where is your love? It doesn't depend on your husband or wife, it depends on you.

Do you have a capacity for respect? Then who are you saving it for? For people who are already so wonderful and impressive that they command respect from everyone? People who have no need of your respect?

It's similar to what people say about believing in God. "If God will just show me some miracles, then I'll believe in Him." What's God supposed to say, "Gee, thanks a lot!"?

That's like the woman who tells her husband, "Show me that you can make lots of money, then I'll stay married to you." Thanks, but no thanks.

Where is your talent? Where is your ability? Where is your virtue? You have a husband? Respect him. You have a wife? Love her.

Everything seems so easy when we first get married. We feel so much excitement in the beginning, because we look at the person we are going to marry, and we can see that there is so much to love and so much to respect, so much to appreciate and so much to admire.

Then, two weeks later, the honeymoon is over. The wife looks at the husband and says, "Why? Why did I marry this guy? What did I ever see in him? How can I respect him? He doesn't do anything to make me respect him!"

And the husband thinks, "What was it I saw in that woman that made me appreciate her? There's nothing worth appreciating!"

So the two of them run to a marriage counselor. The wife says, "I have a problem. I don't respect my husband." And the husband says, "The problem is my wife. She doesn't do anything worth appreciating." Well, they both have a problem, but not the one they thought they had.

The real problem is that their attitude was all wrong. They assumed that if people make you respect them, then that's the real thing; but if you have to put in a little effort, and make believe you respect them, then that's fake. The exact opposite is true.

Look at what happened between the Jews and God.

The Jews felt an initial attraction for God because He was very impressive. When God Himself came in all His glory to take us out of Egypt, we couldn't help but respect Him. We couldn't help but be in awe of Him. We couldn't help but love Him.

When He said, "Come, let's go into the desert," we said, "Sure, whatever You say." He said, "I'll give you the Torah and all the commandments," and we said, "Fine, whatever You say," because we were really impressed with Him. We were really in love with Him.

He took us to Mt. Sinai and we were married. Then He took us to this place called Israel for the honeymoon. It was a long honeymoon; it lasted about four hundred years.

It was wonderful, because Israel is such a holy land. Wherever we turned, we could see miracles performed daily. God was very impressive, and the relationship was constantly being renewed and refreshed. Our admiration for Him couldn't help but grow.

Then God said, "Honeymoon's over. No more temples, no more miracles. No more living in a holy land. From now on, it's just Me and you. If you love Me, you'll have to love Me for what I am, not for my signs, or wonders, or plagues. No more miracles, no more splitting seas. Just Me." So the Temple was taken away, and we were sent out of Israel into Exile.

What happened? Our relationship flourished. Today, in spite of everything, we are as devoted to God as ever. We have shown Him love and respect that we didn't know we were capable of. Feelings that we didn't know existed were revealed.

The same can be true in your marriage.

At the beginning of your relationship, you got carried away because there was so much to love, appreciate, and respect. That wasn't real. That was a gift. A door prize. Just to get you to come to the marriage.

She was wonderful; he swept you off your feet. So you respected each other, you loved each other, and you adored each other. But it wasn't real.

For that you didn't have to be good, or virtuous, or responsible, or moral. You didn't have to do anything. It got done to you. You were completely passive.

The real thing is now. Now that all the excitement has settled down, there are two people who are responsible to one another, who can love each other and respect each other. That's real.

You don't respect your spouse, and you can't live with a person you don't respect? Well, what are you waiting for? Start thinking respectfully, speaking respectfully, and acting respectfully. The same is true of love. You know what love is, because you feel its absence when you're not getting any. Don't sit there contemplating, do something!

One kind thought, one holy word, and one good deed can change the world. So think lovingly, speak lovingly, and act lovingly. By doing so, you will reveal all the love and respect inside you that you never dreamed existed.

Chapter 6
Don't Take Yourself
So Seriously:
Humility and Anger

Just as it is immoral to think, speak, and act in certain ways, it is also immoral to feel certain feelings.

This statement is such a departure from what we generally believe today—that human feelings or human needs can never be wrong—that it can be shocking to contemporary Americans. "What? What do you mean? I have a *right* to my feelings!"

But do you? Some of these negative feelings, such as sadness, arrogance, and anger, are actually destructive forces that serve to undermine our relationships. They are common human feelings, yes, but we can exist and function without them. In fact, our marriages and our relationships are better off without them.

When we say that it's wrong to lose your temper, we're not merely suggesting that being even-tempered might be nicer for your spouse or make you more lovable. We're talking about right and wrong, acceptable and unacceptable. Imagine the following scene:

One day a man attends a business meeting. He's giving his report, when his boss asks him if he's got his facts straight. The man is furious. "What do you mean I've got my facts wrong? How dare you insult me!" Red-faced and shaking, the man storms out of the meeting, slamming the door behind him.

On his way home, he thinks, "If that guy is too stupid to know good work when he hears it, he's not fit for the job. Not only is he too stupid, he's too young. I'm older than he is. For that reason alone, he should have had more respect for me."

He walks along a little further, and then he thinks, "It wouldn't have been so bad in private, but why did he have to disagree with me in front of all those people? Now my reputation is ruined." The more he thinks about it, the angrier he gets.

By the time the man gets home and walks in his front door, he is so upset that he can't answer when his wife asks, "Why are you home so early?" The next day he's still angry, and he decides not to go to work. "I can't bear to look that man in the face."

Now picture the same scenario but with a different man: The second man goes to the meeting, gets insulted, takes offense, makes a big scene, and storms out. On the way home, he thinks, "How could that guy do that? He practically called me a liar in front of everybody."

He walks a little further, then thinks, "If he was going to call me a liar, it should have been about the things I do lie about. But today I wasn't lying; I was telling the truth."

A little further yet: "Sometimes I don't check my facts. I guess it's not so unthinkable that he would be suspicious. How was he supposed to know? Did I have to get so angry?" The more he thinks about it, the more embarrassed he feels.

By the time he gets home, he's too ashamed to explain to his wife why he came home early. The next day, he's embarrassed. "How could I behave that way? A grown man, losing his temper over such a petty thing?"

The first man's anger stems from arrogance; he takes himself too seriously. The second man's ability to dissipate his anger comes from humility; he realizes that his self-interest is insignificant. In fact, anger is a form of arrogance, and both are caused by a lack of humility.

In general, we should strive to be moderate in all things. We should always choose the middle road—not too far to the left, not too far to the right. This center path is known to be the path of truth. But there are two important exceptions to that rule: being humble and avoiding anger. In fact, being humble and avoiding anger are really the same thing.

When it comes to being humble and avoiding anger, we need never be moderate. Then it is appropriate and healthy to go to the extreme. We can be moderate in love, in appetite, in praise, and in the way we spend money, but never in refusing to get angry.

We become angry when we have too high an opinion of ourselves, when we take ourselves too seriously. That's arrogance. But just as none of us is so significant that we have a right to be arrogant, none of us is so important that our anger is justified. Whenever someone hurts us, bothers us, or offends us, and we lose our tempers, we justify our behavior by saying, "Well, he made me angry." We speak about our "right" to be angry, which justifies whatever we say or do, even if we lose control completely. We tell ourselves, "I know I shouldn't act that way, but I was very angry."

Intelligent human beings do not permit in their hearts, in their minds, or in their lives things of which they do not approve. When we lose our tempers and behave badly, we are in perfect control—we are letting it happen.

People often use the same excuse for things they do when they are intoxicated. A man might say to his wife, "I forgot to do what you needed me to do, but I couldn't help it, because I was too drunk." She, on the other hand, could respond, "But I noticed as you were walking down the stairs, you reached for the banister. How come you weren't too drunk for that?"

No matter how drunk we are, certain things remain important enough that we don't forget them. The things we might forget while drunk are only those things that don't really matter.

The same is true of being angry. When we do something wrong, we are letting it happen; we are responsible, not the anger. No matter how justified we might feel, anger is never a justification for bad behavior. But unless we recognize anger as unnecessary and detrimental to the well-being of our relationships, we will never learn to give it up, to let go of it entirely. It will go on ruining our lives, and ruining our ability to have and maintain intimate relationships.

Some people may smoke too much and agree that smoking too much is making them sick, but they will not quit. Others may drink too much and agree that getting drunk is a real problem, but they won't do anything about it. They are convinced that driving drunk is bad, that coming home drunk is bad, that getting drunk four times a week is bad, but they are not convinced that it's bad to take "just one drink." You might say that chain smoking is terrible and you shouldn't do it. But if that's your attitude, you'll never change. Nobody gets up in the morning and says, "I think I'll chain smoke today." You get up in the morning and you smoke one cigarette.

Unless you are convinced that "even one" cigarette is wrong, you're not going to stop smoking. Unless you are convinced that taking "even one" drink is wrong, you are not going to stop drinking. And unless you are convinced that anger is not essential but illegitimate, in any amount, you won't stop getting angry. You'll just find better excuses.

Anger is not an emotion. Anger is a mood in which you're not disposed to any emotion. You don't care about what you say and how you behave; you can't remember whom you love and whom you fear. When you're angry, you can't feel emotion.

The term emotion should be limited to describing feelings that occur between people. Other feelings should be called sensations, moods, dispositions, but not emotions.

A disposition means the general mood of a person that can either encourage or discourage the activities of the mind and heart. Anger is a disposition that prevents emotion; it is not itself a genuine emotion.

Love, for example, is a legitimate, valid emotion. It's a feeling we have toward other people. Hate is also a genuine emotion. It's not good to hate, but it's a genuine emotion because it has to do with someone else. But sadness, arrogance, and anger are not emotions. Someone who is emotionally crippled, and unable to express love, is still able to express anger. That's because anger is not a genuine emotion, but a mood or a sensation. Unlike a real emotion such as love, anger does not need to be preserved, protected, or cultivated. It's simply not necessary; as a human quality, it's completely undesirable.

Anger can discourage thought as well. When you are very angry, you can't even think; it's too all-consuming. So anger stifles both emotion and intellect. Since it's the combination of human intelligence and emotions that makes us truly human and able to serve God, anger, other than genuine moral indignation, plays no role in the service of God.

The ancient sages wrote, "He who gets angry is as if he worshiped idols." During those moments our tempers are out of control, there is no room in our hearts or minds for God; for those moments, we have rejected Him, and that's idolatry.

In fact, by allowing ourselves to become angry, we fail to acknowledge that everything comes from God. We don't stop to recognize God's part in the events that made us angry. In the Bible, when Joseph's brothers arrived in Egypt, knowing that they had sold him into slavery, they were afraid that he would be angry with them. He was not. He said to them, "I'm not angry, because I have no reason to be. You intended evil; you ganged up on me, threw me into a pit, and sold me away. But God intended it for the good. My suffering, my slavery in Egypt, my sitting in prison, my being abused and finally elevated—all of this is God's plan, and that plan is for the good"(Gen. 45:5–8).

The messenger or vehicle of God's will may have ulterior motives, but that's their problem. What is happening to you is coming to you from God. Ask yourself why. Ask yourself what you need to learn from this, what God is trying to tell you. Don't shoot the messenger. Remember that the next time your heart gets set off, and there you are, feeling angry. After the initial rush of feelings, dismiss the anger. Allow your mind to come into control and take over. Rather than fuel the anger, your mind will be able to cool the anger.

Remember Joseph. Without him, without his foresight in the face of drought and his system for storing grain, Egyptians, Canaanites, and Israelites alike would have starved. Instead, his family arrived in Egypt, all were saved, and saved with dignity.

"You thought for the bad," he told his brothers. "But that's between you and God. If you want me to preach to you, I'll preach to you. If you want me to teach you how to be better, I'll teach you how to be better. But angry? I have no reason to be angry."

How is that possible? When something is morally wrong, don't we have an obligation, a moral responsibility to react? Aren't we supposed to object, complain, insist that it stop? It's true that moral indignation is legitimate, but it's appropriate and justified only in the truly moral person, the saintly person who is good all of the time. Only those who live their lives totally devoted to morality and goodness are justified in having a strong reaction to what is immoral. "Anger" on the part of such a person is directed to the immorality of an act or an event. It's not a personal response. As soon as the wrong is righted, the saintly person's feeling of outrage is gone. Unless we are completely righteous to begin with, we have no business being morally indignant.

My teacher used to say, "You have to be consistent. Don't suddenly turn self-righteous on select occasions. If you're not on that level of righteousness, don't pretend to be when it suits you." And then he told me this story:

"There was once a farmer who had one goat in his herd that gave no milk. For years he tried to cure her, but nothing helped. One year a plague broke out among the goats, and the goat that gave no milk came down with the disease. The farmer cried, 'When it came to giving milk, you weren't a goat. Now that it comes to goat diseases, all of a sudden, you're a goat!' "

Moral indignation is appropriate for people who are deeply moral. But if you are careless with your own morality, anger is simply not justified. So, in your marriage, if your husband hurts your feelings, your reaction should not be one of indignation. Your first thought should not be, "How do I get back at him? How do I punish him for this?"

When we are feeling angry, we are wholly absorbed by it. No one and nothing else exists. When we are angry, our spouse doesn't exist, our children don't exist, and God doesn't exist. That's not conducive to intimacy; it destroys the intimacy.

There is never a reason or justification for being so wrapped up in your own sense of self-importance that you exclude your family, your neighbors, your people, or your Creator from your mind, heart, and life.

Chapter 7
Surrender
and Responsibility:
Virtues Essential to an
Intimate Relationship

Surrender and responsibility are inseparable attributes essential to every intimate relationship, including the relationship between God and humankind. We regard our relationship with God as a marriage, and apply what we learn from that to our human relationships. We also look at human marriages and apply what we learn from them to our relationship with God.

Jewish tradition describes the day that the commandments were given at Mt. Sinai as a wedding day. Picture it this way:

Mt. Sinai was held over our heads like a wedding canopy.

The Ten Commandments were the marriage contract.

The precious stone on which the commandments were engraved was the wedding ring.

Moses was the matchmaker.

And heaven and earth were our witnesses.

Then God said to us, "Surrender to me totally, but be fully responsible for your morality. Submit to me completely, but remain accountable for your actions." Wasn't that a contradiction in terms? Complete surrender and total submission seem to rule out responsibility and accountability.

We might think that in order to surrender to God and be close to Him, we have to give up our free will and dissolve into Him. Then celibacy seems holy, perennial fasting a great virtue, forswearing material possessions godly. Maybe we should stop being ourselves because "where God is, nothing else can be."

To ourselves we may say, "God knows what He's doing. God gave me this life and I accept it completely. Without a question. I'm surrendered." We then think of ourselves as deeply religious.

To God we may say, "Whatever You want is fine, I am perfectly content, I will not question Your judgment, I will not fight fate. I surrender to whatever Divine Providence has in store for me. Take me, I'm yours."

The problem with this kind of religiosity is that once we have surrendered, we don't see the need to be responsible. That's like a mother who says to her child, "Fine, have it your way, but if it doesn't work out, don't come to me with your complaints. If you mess up, it's your problem, not mine, because we're doing it your way."

There was once a man who refused to pay his debts, so he was brought before the high court and questioned. The man, a mystic in his own mind, scoffed: "Money, what's money? Money is nothing. Life is nothing. It's all nothing."

The court ruled: "This nothing should be stretched out on a nothing, and given thirty nothings on his nothing." The man promptly decided to pay his debt.

Some people feel that the greater the surrender, the less the responsibility. The attitude is, "Whatever problems exist in this world are God's responsibility because I am powerless. I am nothing."

But it's a mistake to think that way. We ought not assume that the way to surrender to God, to merge with and be connected to Him, is to be self-effacing. The marriage at Sinai tells us otherwise.

In describing the mystical event, Scripture tells us that "God came down on the mountain" (Exod. 19:20). Why the emphasis on "coming down"? Because this was going to be a different kind of revelation, unlike any other that ever preceded or followed.

The revelations described elsewhere in the Bible delivered messages, shared information, or gave instructions. They were meant to be communications. When God spoke to Abraham and said, "Your children will be slaves in a foreign land," He was giving important information, but it was not a "coming down" (Gen. 15:13).

When God told Moses, "Speak to Pharaoh, King of Egypt," He was giving an instruction, but it wasn't a "coming down," either (Exod. 6:11). What made the revelation at Sinai so radically different was not that God spoke—He had spoken before—but that He made Himself vulnerable by surrendering to us. That is what is meant by "God came down."

By giving us free will, the outcome of God's "project"—the world—is at our mercy. We may either keep the commandments or not, because He gave us complete freedom of choice. In fact, the ancient biblical commentaries say that the verse: "If you follow my commandments, I will give to you the rains on time" (Lev. 26:3–4), should be understood as: "Please follow my commandments, and I will give you the rains."

In other words, although God trusts, hopes, and depends on us to keep His commandments, to fulfill the purpose for which He created us; the results are up to us. Therefore He is asking us, pleading with us, to be good.

In doing so, He surrenders Himself. He is our Master and Creator, but He makes Himself vulnerable to us. He is our Provider, our Sustainer, our Helper, our Salvation, and our Hope, but He makes Himself dependent upon our free will.

As much as we need Him, He tells us that He needs us; that is, He needs us to keep His commandments. In that sense, God "came down." In that sense, God became totally surrendered. Yet He remains Master of the Universe, totally responsible. Similarly, we remain responsible for our actions even as we surrender to Him.

There was once a saintly rabbi named Rabbi Schneur Zalman of Liadi. He lived on the second floor of a building, and his son, Rabbi Dov Ber, lived on the ground floor with his wife and baby. One day Rabbi Dov Ber, who was known to have unusual powers of concentration, was so absorbed in a holy text that he didn't hear the baby fall out of the cradle next to him.

On the floor above, the grandfather, Rabbi Schneur Zalman, heard the baby fall. He came downstairs, picked up the crying child, and comforted him. When the child had quieted, the grandfather placed him back in his cradle, and returned to his study upstairs. Later that day he told Rabbi Dov Ber:

"It's good to be so surrendered to holiness that you don't hear the ring of a bell, or a knock on the door. But you must always hear the cry of a child. What's the point of communion with God, if you neglect to do godly acts in this world?

"No matter how engrossed, no matter how close you feel to God, you must never fail to hear the cry of a child. No matter what kind of holy activity you are engaged in, you must never fail to be concerned for another person."

We must remain accountable for the welfare of our fellow human beings. Even at Sinai, at the moment of our greatest spiritual surrender, the Jews accepted the responsibility to observe the commandments. Surrender to God does not exempt us from responsibility.

In everything we do, as we attempt to attain godliness, as we strive to cleave to God, as we surrender to God, we remain responsible parties in a relationship. That's what is meant by our marriage to God.

So in saying, "surrender to me totally, submit to me completely, but be accountable and responsible for your morality," God was telling us how to be married, because surrender and responsibility are essential to every intimate relationship.

The surrender in a relationship never means a surrender of responsibility, but a surrender of ego and self-satisfaction. Many marriages get into trouble because of the lack of surrender.

Ideally, in a strong traditional marriage, the husband surrenders to the wife and the wife surrenders to the husband. No less and no differently. As responsible as the wife feels for the husband, the husband feels for the wife.

The loving grandfather of old was comfortable with whatever craziness, whims, or idiosyncrasies the grandmother had. He had surrendered to her and at the same time felt responsible for her. If she developed a physical infirmity, he never had a word of complaint or resentment. He wasn't heard to say, "What do I need this for? What did I get myself into?" In that kind of relationship, the acceptance of and submission to each other was unconditional, yet neither spouse was self-effacing.

She was good at her job and he at his. They may have communicated on different levels, but in terms of surrender and responsibility, husband and wife were equals. I once knew an elderly couple whose marriage seemed to be terrible, but their relationship was a perfect example of this.

This couple had gone through World War II in Europe, and they were still going through it. For them, the war never ended. The after-effects had shattered their nerves forever. Not only could they not forget the war, they carried it on between them.

She described him as a monster, which was strong language for her to use. They were in their seventies when she decided to leave him. With great courage and self-assertion, she got herself an apartment and moved out. It wasn't an easy decision to come to, but she did it and she loved it.

All of a sudden, my wife and I got a call from her that she had moved back to the house. "What happened?" we asked.

"My husband is very ill," she replied.

"So? What do you mean, 'your husband'? You moved out. He's a monster. You left him."

"But he's sick. He needs me."

The man died soon after. "You know," she said when we went to visit her, "I can't remember the bad parts, only the good parts. There were bad times, weren't there? He was a monster, wasn't he? I can't remember."

Her surrender and her responsibility were total. Underneath the fighting, criticizing, cursing, and screaming, their marriage retained two vital ingredients: the combination of total surrender and profound responsibility absolutely crucial to a relationship.

She thought, "If he needs me, then never mind that I have an apartment that I'm paying for. Never mind that it took me years to work up the courage to leave. Never mind that I enjoy being by myself. He needs me." Total surrender and total responsibility.

Surrender and responsibility, to God as well as in marriage, were the threads that held the Jewish people together, and enabled them emotionally and mentally to survive the darkest periods of their history.

They were the strengths that allowed them to come out the other end, rebuild their lives, raise children, and remain moral and decent human beings.

Total surrender and total responsibility. If we want those strengths for ourselves, we must surrender completely and, at the same time, remain responsible to our relationships.

Chapter 8
Are You Afraid to Surrender? Being Receptive to Another Person

In a relationship, to surrender means unconditional acceptance and total commitment. When the Jews said, upon receiving the commandments at Sinai, "We will do and we will listen" (Exod. 24:7), they meant, "We accept You, God, as You are and we surrender to You unconditionally."

Most people find the thought of unconditional surrender to another person frightening. But surrender in a relationship doesn't mean you say, "OK, you win, I give up, I'll do whatever you want." That may be surrender in battle, but a relationship is not a battleground. Surrender in a relationship means to give up your preconceptions of what another person is, but to remain committed to that person.

In marriage, you have to have the kind of receptiveness that enables you to perceive your spouse as he or she really is. But in order to do so, you must first become open, empty, and very vulnerable.

Many people would like to be this way but don't dare; the thought of being that vulnerable is too frightening. They think, "I can't be so trusting or I might be hurt and taken advantage of. How can I be sure I'm not losing control or surrendering to the wrong person?"

In other words, they are asking, "How do I get a handle on being surrendered? How can I control it, guide it? How can I be sure that I'm not surrendering indiscriminately?" Obviously, surrender requires definition.

The Lubavitcher Rebbe, Rabbi Menachem M. Schneerson, once said to his doctor, who was drawing blood at the time, that a hypodermic needle creates not merely an empty space, but a designated vacuum, drawing in only what was meant to be drawn in. Although a syringe is empty, the Rebbe explained, its very emptiness is "focused."

We need to be like that: "designated vacuums," allowing ourselves to be open, but very specifically, drawing in only what is meant to be drawn in. Just as a hypodermic needle focuses on what is meant to enter the vacuum, so, too, we should not permit ourselves indiscriminate surrender in the sense of abandonment, but "focused" surrender.

The important word here is surrender, so let's take a closer look. Philosophically speaking, everything in this world is both a recipient and a donor, taking in what is above and giving to what is below. Just as every link in a chain hooks into what is above it and slips into what is below it, so all creation receives from what is above and gives to what is below. However, the receiving part and the giving part are opposites.

In order to receive, there has to be an emptiness that allows whatever is going to come in to do so. Giving, on the other hand, requires fullness. A pitcher is better able to pour when full; a cup is better able to receive when empty.

A teacher is better able to give when she's filled with knowledge. A student is better able to absorb when he has emptied his mind and opened himself to the lesson. So, although it seems paradoxical, an empty mind is a receptive mind.

Imagine yourself concentrating on a certain problem. You know what the question is but you don't have an answer. You rethink the question. When the answer continues to elude you, you try harder. As you concentrate, all other thoughts are banished from your mind. You forget you haven't eaten, you lose track of time, you care only about the problem. When the answer doesn't come, your mind goes blank. Even thoughts about the problem vanish, because you've given up. Then, when your mind has surrendered, the answer comes.

As long as your mind hasn't emptied itself, it retains its pre-established conditions. It says, "What you're going to tell me had better fit what I already know, otherwise it won't make sense to me." A mind in that condition is not ready for radically new ideas. By emptying itself, the mind no longer puts any conditions on what it's going to know.

The mind has to surrender completely. It does this by totally nullifying itself, in other words, by creating an empty space. In that empty space, the flash of discovery takes place. A moment later the mind comes back to life, so that the realization will not be forgotten. Within seconds, the mind goes from nonexistence back to existence, back to knowing.

This is revelation. This is knowing. This is creation: something out of nothing. In this emptiness, the mind puts no conditions on what it's going to know. The mind surrenders to the idea and perceives it as it actually is.

In our relationship with God, we can really know Him only when we are completely open to what He is. When we are surrendered, we say, "God doesn't have to be what we want Him to be. He can be who He is, not who we imagine Him to be, or who we need Him to be." Going back to the revelation at Sinai, when the Jews surrendered, they became receptive to truth.

The same is true in establishing an intimate relationship with another person. If you want to allow someone into your life, and accept them as they really are, you have to become open, receptive, and surrendered.

That's the only way you can really know another person, when you are completely open to who they are. A husband should say of his wife, "If I discover that she has needs that I don't understand, that's fine. My devotion is to her, not to what I need her to be, not to what I think she is, nor what I think she ought to be."

But just as the syringe focuses on what is meant to enter its vacuum, so, too, must your surrender in a relationship be *focused*, of a certain designated kind, not generic.

You have to allow yourself to be open, but in a way that is discriminating. If you are indiscriminate in your surrender, if you surrender to anyone and everyone, you have a good reason to be frightened. You are much too vulnerable. If you have no borders or definition to your life, then you have no security either. Discriminating surrender, focused surrender, is the kind of surrender to strive for.

How? By becoming more modest. Modesty means, "focused surrender": that what should come in does, but what needs to stay out, stays out.

That's why "indiscriminate" is another way of saying "immodest." Immodesty means that you are displaying a personal and private part of your being, indiscriminately.

You may do this without being aware of it. You might not say or wear anything immodest, but a certain manner or look in your eyes might demonstrate casual openness and availability.

Modesty may appear to be in conflict with surrender, with openness and receptiveness. When you are modest, it's always: "You can't do this, and you can't do that." It seems stifling and inhibiting, not intimate.

In truth, however, modesty and surrender are not in conflict. Modesty means, "I am not available here, I am not open now. But in the right time and in the right place, in a clearly defined relationship, I can surrender totally."

And then you do. In fact, that's the only way to surrender, the only way to be intimate. The openness is focused, not scattered.

Some people find it natural and easy to "love" other people, but that's not the kind of love that makes a human different from an animal. Such a love is never based on any purpose or thoughtfulness. When it's time for the emotion to be guided and channeled to the proper arena, it refuses to cooperate. Like a wild animal, emotion that has never been subjected to intelligent guidance will refuse to be corralled. And this is the state that leads to fear of surrender. When we have no control in the first place, the thought of surrender is rightfully terrifying.

The emotions of a mature person are molded by intelligence. These are cultivated emotions, focused emotions, not wild and directionless emotions. Emotion, by definition, means a response to something outside of yourself. Human emotions apply properly only to other human beings, or to God.

For example, we may say that a person "loves" food, but that's borrowing a term that applies properly to a human interaction, and applying it where it doesn't belong. We can enjoy food, we can crave food, but love is not the way to describe that craving. It is not the emotion called love.

Our emotions can be either corrupted or elevated. Human love was not created to be without premeditated purpose. So when it occurs indiscriminately and without focus, then it can become corrupt and immodest.

In a modest marriage, love is guided by intelligence and submitted to the authority of the mind. That's called premeditated emotion. Unbridled love, on the other hand, which is never subjected to control, guidance, or purpose, will not respond even when it needs that authority; it won't understand.

The same is true with surrender. If that feeling is not a purposeful one, if it's not a premeditated one, if it's not subject to the control of the mind in its initial birth, it won't respond to reason. If it gets out of hand—and it inevitably will—when you try to bring it back into line, you find that it won't cooperate. It's not accustomed to obeying; it's like a wild growth.

You can use your mind to deal with your feelings and emotions, and train them to respond to intelligence. Then, when it is appropriate to love, you can. When you need to surrender, you can. You'll be able to bring these feelings from deep within your heart when they are needed.

When surrender is inappropriate, you should be able to dispel it, get rid of it and replace it with the feeling that is more appropriate to the situation; and that is modesty.

It's said that the person who flirts with everyone is available to no one. That kind of lack of discrimination is deadly to intimacy, and deadly to marriage. Because marriage is a godly institution, because it engages the divine parts of husband and wife, modesty must be maintained in order to preserve this divine state.

Immodesty destroys it completely. There cannot be intimacy between a husband and wife if they are not modest with each other. Modesty in marriage means sharply focused surrender.

In a modest marriage, the focused surrender is real: not here, not there—now. And when it's now, it's everything. It's total surrender, total naturalness, total spontaneity: total intimacy.

Chapter 9
When It's Healthy to Say "No": How Modesty Creates Borders

Why did God give us the wonderful gift of sexuality and then say, "But don't use it now, or here, or there, but only at this time and under certain conditions"? Why didn't he create sexuality that is perfectly acceptable at all times?

God seems so concerned with what we shouldn't do. We expect Him to be concerned with positive things, such as goodness, morality, holiness, selflessness, charity, kindness, compassion, and so on. But, in Judaism, there are 365 negative commandments and only 248 positive commandments—the "thou shalt nots" far outnumber the "thou shalts." Why does God create certain conditions only to say, "no"?

Because when we say "no" to what is not allowed, to an objective situation rather than to an emotion within ourselves, we establish a protective circle of modesty around us. And within this circle we create for ourselves a private, peaceful place that says, "This is who we are and this is where we belong."

According to Jewish mystical tradition, God also created "a private place" for Himself. The mystics tell us that when God created the world, His light filled the entire existence. He was everywhere; and the physical, finite world as we know it could not exist. So He moved His light to one side, which left an empty space. And in that space God created our world.

The mystics describe this as "a place that was an emptiness." It's a paradox: on the one hand, it was empty; on the other hand, it was a definite place. How can this be?

When we think about it, this idea is really not so unusual. To create a dwelling place in a forest, a lumberjack fells some trees to make a clearing. A city dweller tears down an old, dilapidated house to create an empty lot on which to build a new home. We always need to clear away, to empty an area, before we can begin to build the walls that make our space into a dwelling place.

Here's another example: If you were going to make a cup out of clay, you would have to have an empty space in the middle to contain the water. Then you would need to make sturdy walls to prevent the water from leaking out. Without a space, without walls, it's not a container. It's useless.

So when we create inside of us an "emptiness that is a place," we need two things: emptiness and borders. The emptiness is a place of receptivity and openness that waits to be filled. If we are not receptive, nothing can come in. Then we need borders to define that space. Emptiness without borders is simply a useless void. To create a dwelling place out of emptiness, we need limits.

According to the mystics, God created an empty place, in which He created our world, because He wanted a "dwelling place." A dwelling place is more than a house with four walls, a floor, and a ceiling. It is a place of peace where we can be ourselves, where there's no need for formality. For example, a king would never appear in public without royal garments. But in his dwelling place he can take off his crown and put down his scepter and just be himself.

A dwelling place, then, is a place of privacy. God was motivated to create this world because He wanted a private space. He had the entire universe, of course, but it wasn't private. In order to create a private space, He created our world as we know it: with physical limits, definitions, and borders.

When we set up a life for ourselves and create our world, we follow God's model. We need to create for ourselves a private space, beginning with strong definitions and clearly defined borders. This means we can't have everything. We have to include some things and exclude others. The negative commandments given in the Bible are like the emptiness that God created. Not doing, not yielding to temptations, saying "no" to unhealthy situations is what gives definition to our lives.

If the temptations weren't there, if there was nothing to exclude, then to say "no" would be meaningless. So in order to say "no," we have to have temptations and desires for things that we may not do and will not do.

When we say "no" to unhealthy situations we are building the walls of our dwelling place. When we thus define our inner life we become capable of intimacy. The real meaning of intimacy is that, under certain circumstances, we can invite someone into our private place. We can participate in an interaction, and that interaction will be intimate.

The Bible says there are times when a husband and wife are allowed to be together sexually and times when they are not. Those separations are not a break in the relationship. The separations give definition to the relationship. They are what makes the time together truly intimate: instead of being violated, our privacy is enhanced.

The word for the border that protects our dwelling place is *modesty*. Without modesty, the walls of our dwelling place are already crumbling.

The popular film *Fatal Attraction,* which was one of the top box office successes of 1987, shows how easily such walls can be torn down. It is a chilling vision of what happens when our dwelling space is violated.

The plot is familiar: a happily married man loves his wife and his family. But, one weekend, just for fun, he has an affair with a woman from his office. The woman he sleeps with doesn't understand why she can't become a permanent part of his life.

He says, "I already have a life."

She says, "But I want to be part of it."

He says, "You can't be part of it because my wife's coming home. It was just an affair, okay? My wife was out of town, it was a weekend, and that's all. It's over."

She says, "Should I just fade away, just disappear? What am I supposed to do, turn my back and walk away? Just because she married you first? What about me? What about my feelings? I refuse to be treated like that. I'm not a rag that you can throw out."

He says, "You knew coming into this what my situation was."

Our first reaction is to identify with him and say, "The man is right; leave him alone. What do you want from him? Why are you harassing him?"

Then we learn that she is pregnant. Now her argument is, "You're not facing up to your responsibility."

He says, "It's not my responsibility. You should have been smarter. It's your problem, not mine. Find a doctor and get rid of it."

She can't win. If she agrees, leaves quietly, and has an abortion, we'll think she's an unfeeling monster. If she doesn't walk away, if she becomes clinging and desperate, we'll think she's insufferable.

But she wants to have the baby. She says, "I'm not young anymore. This is your child. I want you to be a father to it. All I want is what I have coming. I want to be part of your life."

He says, "I already have a life."

She says, "Well, I want to be part of it."

He says, "But you can't be part of it."

One day he finds her at his house talking to his wife. The next day she picks up his daughter at school and takes her to the amusement park. He warns her to stay away, and threatens her. She becomes homicidal and comes after his wife with a knife.

Whose side do we take? Who was right and who was wrong? Each of their arguments is logical. She's saying, "You started something. You have to finish it." He's saying, "It was never meant to be that way. It's finished." It's a confusing situation so typical of our times.

When we look at the story from the perspective of modesty, however, it becomes clearer. His marriage is his dwelling place, in which only he and his wife can dwell. He thought he could invite a stranger into that space for a weekend without compromising it.

She had not been installed in his private place, but she can't or won't make that distinction. Perhaps the walls of her own dwelling place are as weak as his. He only has so much to offer; he was only "good for a weekend," but she can't accept that.

The man didn't know where to draw his boundaries; the woman is unable to recognize or appreciate his limits. Metaphorically, the woman represents our passionate nature, and his marriage represents our intimate space. Inevitably, the story ends in tragedy.

Sometimes we're bored in our marriages. We want a little excitement, a little attention. We want to flirt. We don't want to do anything evil, we just want to flirt with forbidden fruit. We justify this need to ourselves by saying, "I don't want to do it, I just want to watch it, I want to read about it, I want to get a little vicarious pleasure from hearing about others doing it." It gets our adrenaline flowing, and we think we can get away with it, since we're only flirting.

Our society is convinced that we can flirt with borders and never really violate them. *Fatal Attraction* points out that we can't. Passion isn't that simple; once we let it in, it won't leave so quickly. Any passion that we have no intention of following through on—any attraction to which we will have to eventually say "no," but with which we toy and pretend—is "fatal." We flirt with it for a while, and when it gets complicated, we kill it.

But if we kill a passionate response, we're killing something that's a part of us. If we let it live, the passion will become an all-consuming monster. It will kill us, gobble us up.

If we create something that we can't conclude, one of two things will happen: either a passion that is never meant to be intimate will become so, which can lead to tragedy; or that which is now intimate will no longer be so, because we violate it.

So in the film, the couple could continue their relationship, which would become deeper, muddier, murkier, and without love. He could decide to leave his wife, or his wife might leave him. Either situation will destroy his dwelling place, and he will be left with nothing, neither wife nor mistress. The woman comes to kill his wife because the passion that she represents is an unwanted intrusion, and such intrusions devastate privacy.

What about permissible, legitimate passion? That passion we are more than willing to go all the way with. On the contrary, we want it to go all the way. We want it to get deeper and deeper and more inclusive, all–inclusive. We want to completely dissolve into that kind of intimate relationship.

We may say "no" to innumerable people; then one person, carefully selected, is allowed into our inner life. Marriage does not compromise our private space, it enriches it. The result is that our passion, our sexuality, becomes more meaningful.

Animals don't say "no." Animals also don't say "yes." They have passions, seasons, and instincts, but they have no "say" in the matter at all. Human beings can say "yes" once because they say "no" many times.

Therefore the restrictions concerning sexuality are not negative; they allow human passion, human sexuality to be a place of holiness. By saying "no" to the wrong situation we create the "yes" to the right emotion.

That's the definition of marriage: permissible, holy passion to which we say "yes," and it does not violate our dwelling place.

Imagine a Martian observing a human building a home. The person whose home is being built is working with anticipation, anxious for his home to be finished. He bangs, saws, and hammers. Finally, all the construction and work are finished. He walks in and what does he do?

He lies down. And now he's happy.

That's it? For this he worked, just so he could lie down?

For that one little bit of comfort, security, and privacy, we have to put up a lot of walls. We have to say "no" to the east, to the west, to the north, to the south, to the top, and to the bottom.

We have to build the walls from bricks or boards and put them together to be solid. We have to make sure that they're not too thick, or no sunlight will come in. We have to make sure they're not too thin, or the wind will come through. If it's going to be our own house, it has to be carefully built.

When our house is carefully built, when we've defined our private place, then there can be passion, intimacy, and human sexuality to which we say, "yes," joyfully and totally.

The Bible tells us in Genesis 28:11 that after leaving his father Isaac's house, Jacob stopped to sleep in a field. Before falling asleep, he surrounded his head with stones. He marked off a place for himself, saying, "I am claiming this as my space. This is the border, the outline, the definition. Within that definition is my place where I belong. Outside is not."

We must have those two parts: "Inside is mine, outside is not." A person can't say, "Inside is mine, outside also." Then there would be no inside, no privacy, no intimate space.

That's what modesty is all about. It is the curtain that marks the transition—the border—from what is not ours to what is ours, from what is not personal to what is personal, from what is not private to what is private.

If we don't appreciate the positive, constructive rewards of saying "no" to unhealthy situations, then saying "no" will feel stifling. But once we realize that modesty represents the walls of our own home, the walls of our private space, then we will appreciate and respect them and seek to keep them strong.

The result is that we will appreciate every moment of passion and sexuality that is allowed. We will be thankful for the opportunity to share our dwelling place with our spouse, and to become part of that person's innermost private life.

Chapter 10
A "New" Perspective
on Dating:
Modest Relationships

I once spoke to a group of high school students about the stresses produced by the social life of most teenagers, and suggested an experiment: a moratorium on coed partying and dating for a month. Their response was immediate: "No way, forget it!" and there was a lot of laughter.

When the class was over, some students spoke to me privately. Away from their peers, they admitted, "I think it's a good idea, and I'd be willing to try it, but I don't think anyone else is going to."

They wouldn't say it in public, but privately they agreed that teenage dating is a stressful, unnecessary burden. The competition, they said, is not fair to the kids who aren't popular; and the kids who are popular become cruel about it. It doesn't do anyone any good.

I wasn't surprised, then, that many of the kids in the class told me they would be more cautious in their relationships and wait for marriage.

It is sometimes argued that dating results in better marriages. The rationale is that exposure to a variety of experiences enables a young person to make a more thoughtful choice of marriage partner.

Few people make that argument anymore, however, because it clearly isn't true. Teenagers have been dating now for several decades. In that time, marriages haven't gotten any better; they've become a lot worse.

The high school students had heard stories of arranged marriages, and were curious about the traditional Jewish way of courtship.

This is what it's like:

Traditional Jews lead a modest social life. Teenagers don't date or go to parties, and boys and girls don't spend time with each other socially. While we're growing up, we don't get into emotional entanglements worrying about how popular we are, or who is more popular, or who we're going to go out with.

None of that happens at all in our community because we think it's unfair. It's not nice, and it doesn't do any good. The result is that when we're ready to get married, we're not playing any games. It's not a popularity contest and we're not trying to impress anyone.

When we're ready to get married, we go about it honestly and sincerely. We don't marry the wrong person because we might have been trying to impress somebody or compete with someone. All that is eliminated. We find somebody to marry, we get married, and the marriages last. Divorces happen, but rarely.

We start to date when we're old enough and serious enough to think about being married. When we do go out, it's with someone who has the same values we do. Usually, we come from families who know each other, or we have a mutual friend who thinks we're compatible and introduces us.

Someone once said, "If you want to marry somebody, and you want to find out what he's really like, what better way than by asking his friends?" The best way to find out what a guy is like, is to find out if he's popular with the guys. To find out how popular he is with the girls doesn't tell you anything. It doesn't tell you what kind of a man he is, or what kind of a husband he's going to be. If you want to find out what kind of a person a woman is, you find out how popular she is with her friends. What matters is what people of the same sex think. That will give you a much better idea of what kind of person she is or he is.

After we are introduced, we spend time together, and we consider marriage. We want to get to know what's on the other person's mind, what kind of life they want to live, what kind of life they have lived, things that have to do with being married. We wouldn't go to a movie because we want to get to know each other, not a movie. We don't want to waste time doing a lot of activities; we prefer to spend the time talking. We're not looking for a thrill; we're looking to get married.

We're not teenagers, so we know much more clearly what kind of person we want to marry. After three or four months, we know if this is the right person or not. If not, there are no hard feelings because we haven't become best friends. If it doesn't work out, it doesn't work out. There's a little disappointment, but no great heartache.

It's a good system, and a considerate system. It takes into account that people have feelings.

For example, in our tradition, while a man and woman are dating and thinking about marriage, the dating is kept completely secret. They don't talk about it and they don't go where people are going to see them. If it doesn't work out, nobody knows.

If it were public, people would wonder, "Why didn't you marry him? Is something wrong with him?" Or, "How come he didn't marry you? Is something wrong with you?" This way is more discreet.

If it works out, everyone is thrilled. If it doesn't work out, no one knows and no one gets hurt.

Men and women who are dating don't touch each other. You would never see a man and a woman kissing or hugging casually. It doesn't happen because this tradition takes male-female relationships seriously. All signs of physical affection take place in private, and are reserved for the person to whom we're married.

In a traditional Jewish home, husbands and wives only touch each other in privacy. Children raised in such a home never see their parents hugging or expressing any kind of physical affection, even playfully.

From this, children learn that family love is structured in two ways: the love between man and woman, and the love between parents and child. That's a healthy message. A hug and a kiss is childish; it's what you do with children. A peck on the cheek is for a baby. Adults have more serious, more responsible, more adult forms of affection.

We're not talking about depriving a child of seeing a happy, healthy relationship between two parents who love one another. We're not talking about any coldness; on the contrary, we're talking about the healthiest and warmest kind of relationship.

A friend once told me about a powerful memory that he had of his parents' affection for one another. The story took place shortly after his family had arrived in America, when he was seven years old.

They were poor, recent immigrants, and they lived in a cellar on the Lower East Side of Manhattan. One night he woke up and heard someone crying. He tiptoed out of his room and looked down the corridor where the dining room was. His mother and father were sitting at the table.

His mother was crying. She was holding a piece of blue paper. His father was across the table from his mother.

He didn't know what the blue paper was, and he didn't know why his mother was crying. At first he was very frightened. But the empathy and closeness between his parents reassured him, and he was able to go back to sleep.

My friend's family had been separated by the war. He and his parents had come to America, but his grandfather, his mother's father, had gone to Israel. The piece of blue paper in his mother's hand that night was an airmail letter notifying her that her father had passed away.

He says he can still picture his parents sitting there, without any physical contact at all. Yet the empathy and the closeness was so real, so palpable, that it could reassure a seven-year-old. He knew it was okay to go back to sleep. That was a very powerful message.

Children who know that their parents care about each other, are there for each other, do what is needed for each other, and respect each other, don't have to see physical affection to know what caring and warmth are.

In a traditional home, parents express a great deal of physical affection toward their children, and privately to each other. But by not displaying their affection for one another in front of their children, they communicate that their husband/wife relationship is different from the relationship between mother and daughter, father and son, brother and sister.

Among traditional Jews, our husband or wife really is the first person and the only person we've ever been this close to, this physical with, and this intimate with, and that's the way it's going to remain. Our husband or wife will always be the only person.

It's a sensitive, considerate, modest, and healthy way to live.

Chapter 11
Your Honeymoon
Should Never End:
How Separation Creates
Fiery Love

There are two kinds of human love: the intrinsic, calm love that we feel for people to whom we're related by birth; and the more intimate, fiery love that exists in marriage. This is why the husband-wife relationship is very different from the parent-child relationship.

The love within a family, between relatives who are born of the same flesh, is innate. The love between a mother and child, a brother and sister, two brothers, two sisters, comes easily. Since they're related by nature, they feel comfortable with each other. There's an innate closeness between them, so their love is strong, solid, steady, predictable, and calm. There's no distance that has to be bridged; no difference that has to be overcome.

The love between a husband and wife isn't like that. Their love wasn't always there; they didn't always know each other; they weren't always related. No matter how well they get to know one another, they aren't alike. They are different from each other physically, emotionally, and mentally. They love each other in spite of the differences and because of them, but there isn't enough of a commonality between them to create a casual, calm love. The differences remain even after they are married, and the love between them will have to overcome these differences.

After all, husband and wife were once strangers. Male is different from female, so in essence they must remain strangers. Because of this, the love between them can never be casual, consistent, or calm.

This acquired love is naturally more intense than the love between brother and sister. When love has to overcome a difference, a distance, an obstacle, it needs energy to leap across and bridge the gap. This is the energy of fiery love.

Because the gap between husband and wife will never really close, their love for one another will continually have to reach across it. There will be distance, separation, then a bridging of distance, and a coming back together, again and again. This sense of distance intensifies the desire to merge.

To come together, man and woman have to overcome certain resistances. A man has to overcome his resistance to commitment, and a woman has to overcome her resistance to invasion. So, in coming together, husband and wife are reaching across great emotional distances, which intensifies their love. The absence of innate love actually makes the heart grow fonder.

If a brother and sister were to have a fiery love, their relationship would suffer. It's not the appropriate emotion for a brother and sister to have. Their love thrives when it's unbroken, unchallenged, constant, and calm. Not that they can't have disagreements, but those disagreements disrupt their love.

On the other hand, if a husband and wife develop a calm love for each other, their relationship will not thrive. If they are too familiar with each other, too comfortable with each other, like brother and sister, their love will not flourish. True intimacy in marriage—fiery love—is created by constant withdrawal and reunion.

If a husband and wife are never separate, their love begins to sour, because they are not creating an environment appropriate to that love. The environment of constant togetherness is not conducive to man-woman love; it's the environment for brother-sister love or parent-child love.

That's why the ideal blessing for a married couple is, "Your honeymoon should never end." A honeymoon—when two people who were once separate come together for the first time—should never end, because that's what a marriage thrives on.

The love between a man and a woman thrives on withdrawal and reunion, separation and coming together. The only way to have an environment conducive to that kind of relationship is to provide a separation.

There are many kinds of separations. A couple can live in different places, have differences of opinion, or get into arguments and be angry at each other. Often the arguing isn't for the sake of arguing, but for the sake of creating a distance so that husband and wife can feel like they're coming together.

That's not a very happy solution. Making up after an argument may be good for a marriage on occasion, but not on a regular basis. It isn't a good idea to go looking for arguments, especially since separations can take a more positive form.

The physical separation given to us by God for that purpose is a much happier solution. That separation is created by observing a collection of laws described in Leviticus as "the laws of family purity," but more frequently referred to as the "laws of *mikvah*" (Lev. 15:19–33). The word *mikvah* refers to the ritual bath in which traditional Jewish women, since the days of the Bible, have immersed themselves following their monthly period and before renewing sexual relations with their husbands.

According to these laws of *mikvah*, during the time that a Jewish woman is menstruating, and for one week afterward, she is physically off-limits to her husband. For those days, the physical separation is total: no touching, no sitting on a swing together, and even sleeping in separate beds.

Through the ages, all sorts of explanations have been given for the laws described in Leviticus, but all of them have one thing in common: Separation protects and nurtures the intimate aspect of marriage, which thrives on withdrawal and reunion.

This understanding is not unique to Jews. In most cultures throughout the world, the ancients practiced varying degrees of separation between husband and wife during the woman's menstrual period. Some, such as certain tribes of American Indians, actually had separate living quarters, menstruant tents, where a woman would stay during her period. Later these customs deteriorated into myths, taboos, fears, superstitions, hygienic arguments, and other rationalizations, in an attempt to make sense of a delicate and sensitive subject.

But separation was such a universal practice that I wonder if human beings know instinctively that male-female love thrives on withdrawal and reunion, on coming together following a separation. The body is actually reflecting an emotional state. Just as the love between man and woman cannot be maintained at full intensity all the time, but needs a certain creative tension without which it will not flourish, the body has a similar need.

As far as Jews are concerned, we know these cyclical changes were created for that very purpose. This is much more than a coincidence: It is how the body reflects the soul, how the body is created in the image of the soul.

Like everything else that exists in our lives, the cycle of withdrawal and reunion that exists in marriage is meant to be a reflection of our relationship with God. The two kinds of love, calm love and fiery love, exist not only among human beings, but between ourselves and God.

When we refer to God as our Father, it's an innate and intrinsic relationship. We don't have to work for it; it's just there. It's a steady, constant love, an indestructible love, a love compared to water—calm love.

But we also talk about how God is infinite and we are finite; God is true and we are not; God is everything and we are barely something. Because of these differences, we feel a great distance from God, and the need to create a relationship with Him. Establishing a relationship in spite of the differences, in spite of the distance, is more like a marriage. That's a stormy relationship—fiery love.

More precisely, our soul loves God like a child loves a parent, because our soul is of God. That love is innate and calm. When God tells this soul to go down into a body, that's a separation. Then our soul loves God with a fiery love, which, like the love between a husband and wife, does not come automatically. Acquired love is by nature intense and fiery.

Eventually, the soul will be reunited with God more intimately than before, just as the intimacy between a husband and wife is deeper when they come together following a separation. Therefore, when God says that a husband and wife have to be modest with one another, that they may be together and then separate, come together and separate again, according to a monthly cycle, it's not an artificial imposition. It may produce discipline, which is nice. It may keep the marriage fresh, which is important. But there's more to it than that.

It is, in fact, the natural reflection of the type of love that must exist between husband and wife. In order to nurture that stormy, fiery love, our way of living has to correspond to the emotions we are trying to nurture and retain.

If there's going to be a separation—and there needs to be one—consider the following: Rather than wait for a separation to develop, where a husband and wife get into a fight or lose interest in each other, let's take the cue from the body and create a physical, rather than emotional, separation.

Everyone is saying, "I need my space." It's true. Keeping the laws of *mikvah,* when they apply, is one way of creating that space; other laws of modesty might be beneficial as well. For example, husband and wife need not touch each other casually or in public; they should avoid casual nudity; and vulgarities, which are inappropriate in mixed company, should also be inappropriate for the home.

In giving us these laws, God tells us: "The marriage love, unlike the family love, unlike the born love, thrives when you separate and come back together. But rather than create an internal, emotional separation, create an external separation by keeping the laws of modesty. Don't separate emotionally; separate physically, and come back together emotionally."

Since the love between husband and wife is one of reaching across distances, of the constant bridging of a gulf, and only that kind of intimate, fiery love is appropriate for husband and wife, our physical behavior has to reflect and support that emotional state. We do that by being modest.

Chapter 12
Are You Thriving,
or Just Surviving?
Three Kinds of Modesty

Everything in creation is meant to thrive in its own environment: Fish live in water, plants live in soil, animals must breathe air. The environment in which a human being thrives is modesty.

But modesty is not so simple. A human being can be modest on three levels: externally, internally, and essentially.

External modesty means your manner of dress, speech, and action, what we usually think of as simple modesty.

Internal modesty means the containment of your inner thoughts and feelings, what we usually call privacy.

Essential modesty is innocence.

On Yom Kippur, the Jewish Day of Atonement, the holiest day of the year, at the holiest moment of the prayers, there is a poetic description sung of the High Priest in the Temple in Jerusalem. His countenance is described as he would emerge from the Holy of Holies, "like a rainbow in the skies, like a rose in a garden, like the grace that shines on the face of a bride groom."

Now, not every bridegroom is beautiful. Why describe the special look on the face of the High Priest as that of a groom? Because a bridegroom who is modest in the way that he is supposed to be—externally, internally, and essentially—reveals his innocence.

That's the object of all modesty: to bring you into contact with your essence, the part of you that is innocent.

Jewish mysticism often speaks of sets of three, and these sets always mean there is an external level, an internal level, and an essential level. Take, for example, the three parts of the soul: The external part is the behavior of the soul—your thoughts, speech, and actions—also referred to in philosophy as the "garments of the soul." The internal part is the psyche—your mind and emotions—called the "powers of the soul." The essential part is the spark of God that is within the soul, the "essence of the soul."

There are also three levels at which we exist as human beings. The external level is the part that's acquired—your habits, customs, behavior, and tastes. These correspond to the garments of the soul. The internal level is the part that's on the inside, the aspect of your personality that's independent of your environment, that makes you really you. The essential level is the part of you that is also part of God.

Your external part changes readily, because its nature is to be vulnerable to influence. You acquire your external being from the outside, so it can be determined by your environment. If you lived in a different society, for example, you would probably dress differently, have different tastes, and hold different opinions.

Your external being is your interactive dimension—how you are affected by other people. The dimension that is on the outside is meant to be that way; other people are supposed to have an effect on you. If the part of you that's supposed to be there for other people were closed, you would have a problem; if no part of you were vulnerable, you wouldn't be human. A certain amount of vulnerability is necessary to be able to function as a human being.

The external part of your being is not "the real you." The fact that you enjoy going to the theater, or buying shoes, or eating fish does not define your inner self. Tomorrow you could choose never to see another play, wear another shoe, or eat another piece of salmon again and you would still be "you."

It is your internal being that is comprised of the traits that make you, "you"—no matter when, how, or where you live, no matter what your environment. If it's your nature to be stubborn, then you're going to be stubborn whether you live in Alaska or Florida. If it's your nature to be flexible, then you're going to be flexible no matter if you're rich or poor. And if you're intellectually inclined, you will be that way if you live in the city or the country.

Children demonstrate their internal being from the minute they are born. They have a unique personality that doesn't come from the outside. Certain character traits are not acquired or learned, but are inborn. Those are the things that are truly "you," your internal person, your inner self.

The internal part of your being doesn't change as readily as the external. It's the real "you," so it's truer. It doesn't fluctuate. It doesn't come from the outside, so it can't be affected or determined by the outside. You can change yourself on your internal level only through effort. For example, if you are not the emotional type, you can work on learning to open up, and become more capable of expressing emotion. A change like this takes effort because you are trying to change the real "you," which doesn't change so easily; but it's still possible.

You can change what you are at the external level fairly easily. With effort, you can change what you are at the internal level. But your essential level can never change.

The external and internal levels are the "created" parts of you, created by God when He created you. But your essential level is not created; it is of God Himself. Because it isn't created, it cannot change, even under extreme circumstances.

These three parts—the external, internal, and essential you—need to be modest in their own ways. Modesty will protect and nurture each of these aspects of your existence.

To nurture your external being, which corresponds to the garments of the soul, you need to be externally modest. This means being modest in your manner of dress and in how you speak and act. Internal modesty means keeping your inner being within, allowing how you think and feel to remain private. Essential modesty means recognizing your innocence, the part of you that never changes, that is not created but is eternal, that doesn't change because it cannot change.

Protected and nurtured, these parts of you do more than survive, they thrive. Immodest people can survive, but surviving is not thriving. They may not die, but if they can't attend to their inner selves, they are not really living, either. Anything that is taken out of its natural environment, that has to contend with hostile or unfamiliar conditions, stops thriving. For example, if you take a shorebird and put it into the forest, instead of eating fish it will have to live on insects. The bird may live, but it won't thrive. It will have to deal with things that distract it from its original purpose.

If you are a gentle person who has to fight off aggression, you can't thrive. Being a gentle person, you thrive on gentle things. If you are not in a comfortable environment, then you are struggling. In order to survive, you are forced to contend with things not of your nature. If you're not using your greatest attribute, gentleness, then you're not flourishing.

You can't live without surviving, but you can survive without living. Survival for its own sake is a distraction from living, and that's when you're not flourishing.

The external you has to have an environment in which external things can thrive. And the internal you has to have an environment in which internal things can thrive. Your skin will flourish when exposed to fresh air, but your spleen will not. Your spleen is an internal organ that can thrive only in an internal environment. Your skin, on the other hand, thrives in air, and would languish without it. Your outer self flourishes in an external environment. For example, your ability to speak, part of your external being, likes to be exposed to company, and flourishes when you're around other people. Your thought is an internal process, part of your inner self. Being surrounded by people is not conducive to good thinking. Thinking thrives on privacy, on being alone. That's its natural environment.

The internal you, the "you are who you are"—your thoughts, your feelings, your individual way of looking at the world—flourishes when you are alone. But the social you flourishes when you are surrounded by other people.

Sometimes you find yourself trying to divide your time and energy between these two environments. You try to create moments when your social skills can flourish, and moments when you can be private so that your inner self can flourish. Celebrities carry this to the extreme. They go out into the social world, fully exposed, and flourish for a month. Then they have to withdraw. They block everyone else out, put on a blindfold, and get headaches. They can't handle phone calls; they're cracking up. They retreat completely into a shell for about a month, rebuild themselves internally, and then they're back out into the open again.

That's not a healthy or happy solution. That's not thriving; that's surviving. A human being is not a collection of pieces, but a harmony of parts. Thriving means that you nurture your external and internal selves at the same time.

How? By being modest. Modesty means there is harmony among the different levels of your existence. With modesty you can create an environment for your external being that is not to the detriment of your internal being. If you are modest, all of you interacts in harmony; all of you flourishes.

By behaving modestly, you can speak, dress, and interact with other people, while shielding your inner self. You can be private for the part of you that needs privacy, and at the same time, social for the part of you that needs company.

That's how external modesty—modesty of speech, dress, and action—protects and nurtures the internal self. When you are externally modest, you become more modest internally. It may seem strange to people who are unfamiliar with it, but in a traditional Jewish wedding, the bride and groom will leave the wedding canopy without so much as a glance at each other. He may be mobbed by the men, she by the women, but between the two of them, in public, nothing is exchanged. Not a glance or a look, nothing. Instead, they withdraw to a room together, where they can be private.

That's internal modesty. Whereas not hugging or kissing in public constitutes external modesty, internal modesty means, "Our inner feelings remain our own. Nobody is going to stand there watching while we express what we feel for each other. Whom we love, what we love, how much we love, is not for public display."

In the Russian village of Lubavitch, the eminent rabbi Sholom Dov Ber was once gravely ill. His little boy, his only child, sat by the door to his father's room day and night. One day the doctor emerged from the rabbi's room with a sober expression that frightened the boy.

The child, who would one day be known as the Frierdicher Rebbe, Rabbi Joseph I. Schneersohn, ran to his teacher to ask what he could do. The teacher said, "Tomorrow morning you will awaken very early and come with me to the cemetery. There I will tell you the prayers and psalms to recite at your grandfather's grave. We will both fast tomorrow, but you must tell no one."

The next morning the little boy arose while it was still dark, left his house, and joined his teacher. The snow was deep in Russia in the middle of winter. The child struggled to walk in the teacher's tracks.

At the cemetery, he burst into tears and pleaded with his grandfather to intercede with the Almighty to save his father's life. As the dawn was breaking, the teacher tapped him on the shoulder and said, "It's time to go back."

When they approached the town, they heard a shout. "The fever has broken. The rabbi will recover." The child looked at his teacher, who said, "Thank God. But remember that this is a fast day for you. And no one must know."

Once again the child waited outside his father's room. When the doctor allowed him in for a few minutes, it was the first time in many days he had seen his father.

His father spoke. "Have you had your tea this morning?"

The little boy was in a dilemma. He couldn't lie to his father. And he couldn't divulge that he was fasting. So he stood there, silent. Fortunately, the doctor entered to tell him it was time to leave.

This child's ability to remain silent demonstrated a profound degree of internal modesty. That he had fasted for his father's recovery remained private.

When you achieve that degree of internal modesty you become receptive to your essence. What is that essence? Innocence.

You can't change your essence, because a person's innocence never varies. All people have the same amount of innocence. However, the innocence can show more in some people than in others, because they reveal it.

Since no one has more or less innocence, a modest person is not more innocent than an immodest person. But she is more in touch with her essence; her innocence is more revealed. Modesty means that you become a vessel receptive to innocence. External modesty, modesty of dress, speech, and actions, is the preparation of the vessel; internal modesty is the vessel, in which the essence is received and contained. By being modest, externally and internally, you touch your essence and receive it. In that way, you reveal your innocence.

Your essence, your essential self, compels you to seek innocence because you are innocent; to choose morality because you are moral; to serve God because, at your very core, you are a part of God.

Chapter 13
"Do You Know Where You Belong?": Three Kinds of Shame

When God first created the world, there was a certain divine sameness to all things: "And God saw all that He had made, and behold, it was very good" (Gen. 1:31). In this world of sameness, Adam and Eve were aware that they were naked, but felt no shame.

After eating from the Tree of Knowledge—and it was a tree of knowledge, not of ignorance—Adam and Eve felt ashamed. What kind of knowledge could have caused this change in their perception of the world?

The fruit of the Tree of Knowledge gave Adam and Eve the ability to make distinctions. Whereas before the world seemed one-dimensional, now it had many dimensions.

In this new world of contrasts, all things were not the same. Some things were personal, others were not. Some things were private, some public. When they looked at themselves, they saw that they were naked—that is, they saw that without clothing, there was nothing to distinguish what was private about a human being from what was public. Their new awareness of the need for clothing caused Adam and Eve keen discomfort. That feeling of discomfort was shame.

The sense of shame that originated with Adam and Eve was a healthy development. It gave them the ability to make distinctions: between private and public, modest and immodest, moral and immoral. Shame means that we recognize these borders. Shame is an essential part of God's plan, because it is the means to retaining innocence.

The first human beings felt three kinds of shame: humility, embarrassment, and guilt.

After eating from the Tree of Knowledge, Adam and Eve felt a kind of shame similar to the shame that comes from having done something wrong; because they were able to see the contrast between God's greatness and their own smallness, they felt small and insignificant. We call that aspect of shame humility.

Humility is what you feel when you're in the presence of someone who is superior to you. He may not criticize or embarrass you, but the very fact that he is much greater than you can make you feel small. And that is shame in a positive sense.

In the days of the Temple, there was a sage who was riding down the road on his donkey. Off to the side of the road he saw a man who appeared to be exceedingly ugly. The sage stopped and said, "Why do you seem so incredibly ugly?"

"Don't complain to me," the man retorted, "complain to my Maker."

The sage had recognized that the man was totally self-centered, and that he was really disfigured by his lack of humility.

The sage used the man's ugly appearance to teach him humility in a very successful way. He said, "Excuse me, but why do you seem so ugly?" as if to ask, "Do you take credit for that, too? Did you make yourself ugly?"

When the man said, "Don't complain to me, complain to my Maker," he was really saying, "I didn't do this, my Creator made me this way. My Creator is responsible for the way in which I appear to you. I don't run the world. I'm not responsible for everything. God is doing this to me; what am I supposed to do?"

For the first time in his life he felt humble; for the first time in his life he was admitting his dependence on the Creator.

That's why, when Adam and Eve felt humility, it was a healthy development. Before eating from the Tree of Knowledge, when the world still appeared to them as one-dimensional, they had not felt the contrast between the Creator and themselves. Now, for the first time, they realized the difference between "small" and "great."

The second aspect of shame Adam and Eve felt was embarrassment.

Like the bumps on a highway that you feel when you're weaving out of your lane, embarrassment is a warning sign telling you that you crossed a border, that you are trespassing. If you accidentally stray out of the proper lane, you are ashamed and you feel embarrassed. This kind of shame, this feeling of embarrassment, pushes you to go back where you do belong.

Just as fear is a warning that danger threatens, shame and embarrassment are the warning of a border being crossed: the border of privacy.

Before they ate from the tree, Adam and Eve were naked. But they felt no embarrassment because they recognized no distinction between "private" and "public." Gaining the power of discernment meant realizing the difference between themselves and their surroundings. For the first time, they had a sense of privacy. They were uncomfortable and embarrassed when they realized that their privacy was violated by their own nakedness. They had been caught on the wrong side of the border.

Then God came to them and said, "Where are you?" What He meant was, "Where are your borders?

"Do you know where you belong? Where don't you belong? Are you where you belong? Are you not where you belong? Where are your borders?"

Then Adam and Eve took fig leaves to cover up their private parts because if you want to strengthen your borders, you increase your modesty.

The third aspect of shame is guilt. Guilt is the inner response that lets you know a relationship has been violated. It's the feeling of despair that you get when you think that a relationship may never be the same again. For example, if you unintentionally hurt your best friend's feelings, you wonder if things will ever be the same again between you. The truest expression of the emotion of guilt is, "Can you ever forgive me? Am I as acceptable to you as before?"

We're talking here about the emotion of guilt, not the legal definition. *Feeling guilty* is not the same as taking responsibility for an act. To find you legally guilty, or responsible for an act, a court of law has to prove that you knowingly and maliciously perpetrated that act, that what happened can be traced to your decision, choice, or action.

This is not so with guilt feelings. Here, the guilt you are feeling means "damaged" in the eyes of others. For example, if a human being handles certain species of animal young, the infant may be shunned by its parents because it now carries the human scent. The animal is not guilty of a crime, but might feel blemished. Likewise, you may *feel guilty*, ie., your relationships with your parents and spouse may be damaged or blemished, by a crime committed against you, such as rape or sexual abuse.

This emotion of guilt can occur only in the context of a relationship. In order to feel unacceptable, you have to feel unacceptable to someone. If nothing happened to violate a parental or spousal relationship, you're not feeling guilty; there isn't anyone to be guilty to.

When you've done something wrong and you're feeling guilty, it's because you're thinking, "Someone told me not to, but I did," or "God told me it was wrong, but it happened." It's not that a law was violated, but that a relationship was violated; not that a commandment was ignored, but the Commander.

That's why you can feel guilty even when you know that what happened was unintentional and not your fault. In spite of the fact that you weren't responsible for the abuse, if your relationships with close friends and relatives were damaged, you feel damaged and you'd like to straighten things out. What you are feeling is the need to be able to be close to them once more.

When you know which relationship was violated, then you can say, "I'm really unchanged. I'm still yours." If you didn't know which relationship was damaged, but you had some vague feeling of guilt, you wouldn't be able to resolve the feeling. That's when guilt becomes never-ending, pointless, and unhealthy.

In such a case, you try to forgive yourself, and that doesn't make any sense. How can you forgive yourself? Besides, you're much too harsh on yourself. You'll never really forgive yourself, but you'll do a good job of punishing yourself. The result is that you're just out to get yourself; what you're feeling is self-destructive, but you're not experiencing legitimate guilt.

If you want to help an abused person who's feeling guilty, don't try to convince him that he shouldn't feel that way. Instead, try redefining that feeling for him as damaged or unworthy.

This may explain why most children and many adults experience guilt following an abusive experience. They may say that they feel guilty even though they do not expect to be held responsible or to be punished. However, they may expect to be rejected by their loved ones.

This is especially true in the event of sexual abuse. If a child feels guilty for what happened, don't deny the child that guilt. Children who have been sexually abused don't need you to confirm their innocence; they need help understanding their sense of loss and what to do about it.

If a child feels guilty—and most children who have been molested do feel guilty—allow the child that guilt but help her to identify and define it.

By giving her the right to her guilt, you will be able to move her on to the healing process. By allowing her to feel shame—humble, embarrassed, and guilty as we have defined it—she can then work on restoring her innocence. Shame is the road to her innocence.

One day a woman came to talk to me. She had been sexually abused from the time she was nine until she was fifteen. Years of therapy had not helped her resolve her feelings of guilt and shame. The therapist had tried to convince her that since she wasn't responsible, she shouldn't feel guilty.

She said to me, "Of course I know that it wasn't my fault and I'm not responsible, but still I feel guilty."

I said, "You really mean 'unacceptable.' The guilt that you are feeling is a sense of loss. You're asking, 'Am I as acceptable now as before? Can I still be loved? How will the people in my life treat me now?' "

You would think that she'd have had an extremely negative reaction, but she didn't. Nothing of the sort. She said, "You're right, I knew it all along. They're trying to convince me that my feeling isn't legitimate, but it really is."

She sounded relieved to say it. Then she asked, "What am I supposed to do now?"

I said, "Let's talk about what feeling guilty really means. If a relationship was damaged, that feels like guilt. If you can identify which relationship you feel was damaged—that with your parents, friends, or future husband—then you will have identified the guilt.

"The feelings you are experiencing are really very healthy. First of all, you now feel small, humbled, and fragile. You know that you need the support of your family, friends, and God.

"Second, you're feeling embarrassed. Your privacy was violated, trespassed, cheapened. You need to have it back, intact, restored, to feel safe. You can do that by strengthening your observance of modesty.

"And finally, you are experiencing the sense of guilt. You feel estranged, alienated, unworthy, and despairing. You feel that your innocence has been lost, never to be regained. You question whether the people in your life will ever be able to accept you after what has happened to you. Your relationships need strengthening.

"If you ask your family or your husband if they still love you, and they tell you that they do, believe them. If you ask God to forgive you, and to accept you as you are, He will. And in doing so, you become innocent, whole, and unviolated once again."

The only legitimate meaning of repentance is to repair a relationship that was in some way violated and damaged, whether with God or with another person. In doing so, we become as innocent as before the relationship was damaged. The three parts of shame are the way we get there; shame is the road that leads us to innocence.

We know from experience that when such an attempt is made to regain innocence—no matter what had happened before, no matter how long the innocence had been lacking—it is regained in a very short time. Regardless of the reason for feeling ashamed, as soon as we ask for forgiveness, we are once again as innocent, as unviolated, lovable, and acceptable as we were before the event.

We must believe that innocence can never be lost entirely. At any moment, and under all circumstances, we are forever capable of regaining our innocence. We are able to undo all the damage, and become once again healthy, whole, and innocent, because we have within us a place of innocence that never gets violated.

When the Children of Israel made the golden calf, the men threw their gold into the fire and out came the idol. To atone for the idolatry, they were told to create a Holy Sanctuary, for which they would need a large quantity of gold (Exod. 25:8; 35:5).

The sages ask, "Where did they get this additional gold from? Hadn't they used it all up on the golden calf?"

The sages answer, "From the women, who had never given any of their gold for the idol in the first place, and from the special gold the men had not relinquished."

There was a fine gold, the sages tell us, that the men kept wrapped in a cloth in their bosom pocket. This gold they would not give for the golden calf. They gave their ordinary gold, but they kept the fine gold near their hearts, and would not part with it. That gold remained available for building a sanctuary, a place for God.

Ordinary gold represents our emotions, but the fine gold represents our innocence. Even if we violate the morality that was given to us by God, and seem to lose our innocence, that loss can only go so deep. Deeper than that, our innocence, like the fine gold, remains intact, always available to us. And we need our innocence.

Without innocence we don't function properly. Our feelings of guilt and shame tear us apart. We're out of balance. A loss of innocence can ruin us because it's not how we were meant to be.

It's innocence we're looking for, innocence we need, and innocence we can have in our lives, when we allow healthy shame—humility, embarrassment, and guilt—to help us remember where our borders should be.

Chapter 14
Creating a Sane Environment: Protecting the Sexuality and Innocence of Children

We hear a lot about child abuse. It seems that half the people we meet have been abused as children. How could this happen? And what is happening on a deeper level? Traditional Jewish teachings can help us explore and understand these questions, and can help us raise children who know how to live modestly in the world.

Psychiatrists say that children who have been sexually abused will typically have a recurring nightmare: The child is running down a long corridor, panic-stricken, trying door after door, until one opens and is welcoming and comfortable. What is the meaning of this dream?

It means, "There's a door that leads to my room, my space. When that space has been violated, I run from door to door trying to find my room again, because the place that had been mine has become public. It was violated, entered without my permission, treated as if it weren't mine. Now I'm looking to find my room again, my place."

What is meant by "my place"? To a child, "my place" means "my modesty."

Children are born with an innate sense of modesty. Even certain animals will not mate if they don't have a place to hide. That animals can be modest reveals that modesty is innate in some creatures; it's a fact of nature, and not the product of higher values or noble ideology. In human beings, it's a natural instinct. That's why when a child is abused, what has been violated is the child's inborn modesty. A child who is abused as an infant, even if no violence or pain is incurred, will later show symptoms of abuse.

What could a one-year-old child know about ethics or inappropriate sexual behavior? An infant can't tell the difference between what's moral and what's immoral. Yet it's clear that such a child feels violated. What has been violated is his or her modesty.

A woman had been engaged to be married three times, and had broken off the engagement every time. Now she was about to be engaged for the fourth time, and she wondered what was intimidating her each time she came close to marriage.

It turned out that when she was young, her father used to come down to the breakfast table wearing only undershorts. She remembered being so embarrassed by this, feeling so uncomfortable with this as a child, that the thought of living with another man who might do the same was too distasteful.

She may have been a very sensitive child with a strong sense of modesty. But children have an innate modesty that is easily violated—and that results in trauma.

A man confided to his rabbi, "I don't know how far I should go in trying to make friends with my stepdaughter. It's been three years now and she won't let me near her. When do I just throw in the towel and say, 'I quit!'?"

"How old is this girl?" the rabbi asked.

"Fifteen," the man replied. "She was twelve when I married her mother. Why is she so cold to me every time I try to be friendly? What's wrong with the girl?"

"Nothing's wrong with her," the rabbi explained. "A fifteen-year-old wants her privacy. You're imposing on her.

"She's trying to tell you, 'You're not my father. I have a father, even if I don't know where he is. I may hate his guts, but that doesn't make you my father, either. So I don't want you walking into my room, and I'm not comfortable having you put your arms around me. I don't want it, and I don't like it. It's an invasion of my privacy, of my modesty.' "

His stepdaughter felt violated not necessarily out of an understanding of sexual ethics, but out of her innate sense of modesty. A door was opened that should have remained closed; a border was crossed that should have remained inviolate.

A woman had an eight-year-old daughter from a previous marriage. One night her daughter came crying to her, saying, "Mike and I were talking in my room, and he began touching me." The woman called the police, threw her husband out of the house, took her daughter to counseling, and began divorce proceedings.

Rather than the long, gut-wrenching discussions with her daughter about sexuality, the facts of life, and the perversions of some men, the woman should have said to her, "It was immodest, and it was wrong." She should have told her husband from the start "You have no business being in her room." Her husband was not allowed to be there alone with his stepdaughter, even if he were Moses. The violation that occurred didn't begin when the stepfather touched the girl. It began when he walked into the room. The problem was not perversion; the problem was immodesty.

In ancient times, it was acceptable for a man to be sexually attracted to a young girl, as long as he made her his wife. It wasn't a perversion then and it's not a perversion now. To be attracted to a thirteen-year-old girl is not abnormal, but to follow through by actually having sexual relations is a crime, and a serious breach of modesty.

It doesn't make sense to say that any man who has a sexual attraction for a thirteen-year-old girl is a pervert, when both of their great-grandmothers may have been married and bearing children in their early teens. Some of the most holy and pious women throughout history had their second child by the time they were fourteen. Were their husbands perverts?

As long as there have been human beings, human beings have had sexual desires for what they may not have. To be aware of the sexual possibilities inherent in every relationship is not sick; it's a mark of humanity.

We need to remember that this is God's world, and He created many nice things in it. Some of them he lets us have, and some things we can't have because they aren't ours to have.

When God created Adam and Eve, He told them, essentially, "You will be tempted by what you may not have, but if you indulge, that's a sin" (Gen. 2:17). Not a perversion. Not a sickness. Not an addiction. A sin.

God never said, "Don't be a pervert." There's no such commandment in Scripture. What He said was, "Be modest, and keep your hands to yourself." You may call a sin a perversion because it perverts God's plan, but it is not a perversion of human nature.

Whether one's attraction is to a married woman, or to one's mother, or to a child, it is normal, natural sexuality. But it is a sin—natural, but not allowed—because it violates God's commandments.

To call sexual misbehavior a perversion of human nature is a failure, a moral failure; you would be choosing a medical objection over a moral one. And for immorality, there is a moral answer: Modesty. Modesty is the only answer.

Laws, in any society, aren't intended for deranged people who are out of control. Likewise, the commandments in the Bible are for normal, healthy people who might be tempted to do what

God says not to do. Why does God prohibit some acts, while allowing others? We can only guess. But disobeying the laws of modesty should not be called a disease. It should be called what it is: immodest and immoral.

Therefore, an adult who is attracted to a child should treat that attraction the same way he treats any other physical attraction that is off-limits: It's a normal, human sexual attraction that is immodest and prohibited.

In our society, we deny the sexuality of children. But Judaism does not deny it. For that reason, regarding sexual abuse, we make a radical suggestion: "Don't call it '*child* abuse.' "

It is abuse, but the abuse that occurs, the violation, has very little to do with the fact they are *children*. In sexuality, as in all other things, every human being has a threshold. Every person who is sexually overwhelmed is violated. Whenever abuse occurs, whether to an adult or to a child, someone is made forcibly aware of a level of sexuality that is too much, that is overburdening mentally, emotionally, and physically.

Sexual abuse is wrong; it's hurtful, and it's devastating. But it's as hurtful and devastating to a twenty-year-old as to a three-year-old. And it's just as immodest.

It's a myth in our society that children are so innocent that they cannot arouse sexual attraction. Modern studies confirm what the ancients knew all along, that sexuality exists at every stage of development, even in newborns. Yet in spite of the evidence, when it comes to the realities of our behavior, we make believe it isn't there.

A photograph was released to newspapers all over the world showing a leading religious figure watching teenage girls in a gymnastics performance. He was watching from a special seat set up for him and seemed to be enjoying the spectacle very much. Yet the same religious figure would never have considered watching adult women perform.

Why would his followers release such an embarrassing photograph? Certainly not to show their leader to be a lecherous pervert. They believed that watching teenage girls exercise in tights and leotards was innocent, without sexual overtones. But who are we kidding? For all intents and purposes, these young girls were women. We make a mistake if we pretend that children are asexual.

That's why to say to a child, "You have a right not to be abused," is nonsense. Even worse is, "You have a right not to be touched by someone you don't want touching you." What about the child who wants to be touched? It happens. Very often the child cooperates, not expecting to encounter adult sexuality.

That's how a child becomes a victim of pornography. It almost invariably happens very slowly, gradually, imperceptibly.

First there's a little immodesty, and then the adult, usually a trusted friend or relative or neighbor, might take a few liberties. The child might not think it's so terrible, especially if he's seen something like it at home, in magazines, or on television. Then the adult may go on to the next step, and the next.

By the time the child realizes there's a problem, the problem is no longer immodesty; it may be pregnancy. Or violence. Or kidnapping. And that's much harder to explain to a child than immodesty.

We're afraid to say up front that touching children in an immodest way is immoral; so we skirt the issue by telling them they have "rights." But you should never say to a child, "You have a right to what you want." By telling children that it's up to them, we blur the line between right and wrong, between modesty and immodesty, between moral and immoral.

You should say instead, "This is right, it's modest, and we're allowed to do it. This is wrong, it's immodest, so we're not allowed to do it."

The modesty with which all children are born should be strengthened and encouraged, so that as soon as another child or an adult makes the slightest attempt at immodesty, the child will know that something is wrong, long before the situation becomes dangerous. Modesty is something children need to know for themselves.

We can talk to children about modesty and immodesty without introducing unwarranted, unnecessary and unpalatable adult subjects. Therefore, what we need to do, what we must do, is teach children modesty from a very young age, even before they are old enough to repeat the word.

How do you teach children about modesty?

First of all, begin by teaching them to dress, speak, think, and act modestly, just as they see you, your spouse, and the other important adults in their lives doing.

Second, teach them that the same restrictions that apply to all male-female interactions apply to adult-child interactions: because from the standpoint of human nature, children and adults are equally sexual beings.

What are these restrictions? That a man and a woman who are not married and not closely related by birth should not touch each other, and should not be locked alone in a room together. This includes adult-child interactions.

If modesty becomes a way of life in your home, your children will get the message. Then, even when they're exposed to immodesty outside the home, on billboards, in magazines, on the television, or at a friend's house, they will at least have a definition.

They will know, "This is immodest. It's something we don't do at home." They will know that it's wrong, they will have a handle on it, and they won't allow it to go too far.

Children who are clear about the difference between modesty and immodesty will know to draw the line, will know what misbehavior is long before it becomes dangerous. They'll be able to identify it, talk about it, and deal with the situation, because they know what modesty is all about. They'll want to talk to you about what happened. And because modesty is something you've discussed before, you will know what to say.

What should you say to a child who has already been the victim of an adult's immodesty?

The only truly relevant, honest statement to make to the child is that what happened was immodest. That's exactly what it was. It was wrong and inappropriate. That's something a child can handle.

What you should not do is go into a panic, sit the child down, and give him or her a crash course on Perverts and How to Avoid Them. You will confuse the child by introducing unnecessary subjects.

Saying that the person who did this had emotional problems would be beside the point. It has nothing to do with the trauma the child experienced. Saying that the police will arrest and punish the offender is not enough.

Tell the child instead that the person who did it was not a modest person, and immodest people should be avoided. Remind the child that in your home, in your family, you observe modesty, and that it's best to remain at all times with other people who are modest.

The laws of modesty were given to us because they are necessary, they make sense, and they are effective. Teaching these laws and observing them will preclude most sexual abuse from occurring. If it should occur, God forbid, modesty gives both adults and children the tools to deal with the situation. Anyone with a strong sense of modesty will know that something is wrong long before it becomes traumatic, and will be able to talk about what happened.

Teaching children modesty at a very young age can only ennoble their lives, make them more sensitive, stronger, and better protected. We don't need to traumatize them or say, "There are perverts out there who are out to get you." We don't need to scare them by telling them things they are not ready to hear, don't want to hear, and are better off not hearing. Let's teach them modesty instead.

There's a light in the eyes of children who know what modesty means, that isn't there in children who know nothing about it. There's an innocence there and a buoyancy that is lacking in children who "know too much," who have been told the wrong things, and not been told the right things.

In giving us modesty to live by, God keeps us sane. By giving us sane laws He allows us to remain light when all else is dark. If we live our lives the way we are meant to, if we teach our children as we are meant to, then that light will shine in our homes.

Simply by living the way God wants us to live, we can create a sane environment. And a sane environment is a good place to raise a child.

Chapter 15
When Saying "No"
Can Be Deadly:
Protecting Our Sexuality

Not long ago, a group of teenagers asked me how to keep kosher while on a canoe trip. *Kosher* usually refers to what food is permissible under Jewish law, and that's, of course, what they meant. Should they take trail mix or dehydrated omelets? But more broadly, as everybody knows, kosher means something's okay to do.

"Who's going on this trip?" I asked them.

"Four boys and four girls."

"I can't help you," I said. "It's already not kosher."

"What do you mean?"

"Four boys and four girls going off into the wilderness on a canoe trip is not kosher!"

These good, clean-cut kids were offended. "We've been doing this for years, we grew up together, we went to kindergarten together. Every year we go on this canoe trip and we don't misbehave. In fact, sometimes we even share sleeping bags."

"In that case, you don't need to see a rabbi," I told them. "You need to see a shrink. You're in big trouble!"

When teenagers can casually dismiss the sexual side of a male/female relationship and claim to be "just friends," it's not a virtue or an accomplishment; it's a sad loss. And what we have lost is our ability to be naturally sexual.

A human being is always a sexual being. What we do with our sexuality depends on who we are, on what we were raised to believe, on how we were taught, and on our society. But we all have one thing in common: Each of us is aware of our own sexuality, unless we stifle that awareness.

A man and a woman alone together is a sexual event—even if nothing else happens. According to Jewish tradition, a man and a woman who are not married to each other, and who are not blood relatives, may not be alone together in a room in which the door is locked. This applies to every man and to every woman. Moses himself being alone with Sarah, wife of Abraham, would constitute a sexual event.

Why would people as moral and ethical as Moses and Sarah need to have such rules? Didn't God think that decent people could be trusted to behave themselves?

Clearly, it's not a question of misbehavior. We're not saying, "We can't leave those two alone in a locked room. Who knows what might happen?" We'd never suspect Moses or Sarah of misbehavior, or even of an unholy thought. Nevertheless, their being alone together would be a violation of modesty.

The very fact that we find this so difficult to understand is an indication of how dulled our sexual nature has become. This dullness of feeling is what enables young men and women to sleep together without acting on sexual feelings. It's fashionable today to say, "There's no difference between boys and girls," as though that lack of difference is a virtue. But it's not a virtue, it's a symptom of disease. Whenever a man and woman are together they should experience a certain awareness of sexuality. If there's no awareness, something is very wrong.

We're certainly not hiding sex in our society. We talk about it, we do it, we see it in movies, on television, in magazines. But for all our talk and openness, our capacity to be sexual is suffering. When we need to be sexual, when it is integral to the success of our marriages and to our lives, we need sex therapists to train us.

Our dysfunction certainly isn't due to lack of practice. Shouldn't people who are liberated and experienced be more skillful? Birds and bees don't have to go to school to learn what we have to go to school for. Something isn't working.

We used to assume that if a man and woman shared a sleeping bag, human nature was such that something happened whether they intended it or not. Of course, it's possible to be so disciplined that teenagers who are "just friends," who are attracted to one another while sharing a sleeping bag, manage to behave themselves. It's possible, but it requires an impressive degree of self-control. And that's exactly how repression occurs.

Kids pay a high price to maintain these "close" relationships: They kill their sexual personality in order to refrain from extramarital relations. And if they kill their sexuality in one relationship, it may be dead for all their relationships.

How many times can we say "no" to our own instincts before our instincts realize that they're unwelcome? If the sexual presence in a relationship is strong but we keep ignoring it, if we maintain the relationship but constantly reject the sexuality, in the end we lose our ability to be sexual.

Sexuality is an ability. It must be protected and cultivated, not denied or exploited. If we stifle our sexuality over and over again, we can't retrieve it when we need it: in our marriages. No wonder sex therapists are making money.

Most therapists who treat sexual dysfunction give their clients this advice at the beginning of therapy: "Don't touch each other for two weeks." Ironically, this advice is given to us in the biblical book of Leviticus for free. Loosely translated, it reads: "Don't touch each other. Then, with the right person, at the right time, and in the right place, you can be sexual" (Lev. 15:19, 25, 28; 18:1–30; and 20:18).

Don't touch each other? Don't even shake hands? Shaking hands is sexual? Yes, it really is. Think about it for a minute. The average person can feel very embarrassed by shaking hands. If a woman shakes hands with a man, and he holds it a second too long, she begins to feel uncomfortable. Was it just a handshake? Or did he intend something more personal?

In the tradition I was born into, and in which I live today, men and women don't shake hands with each other. They do not allow themselves to be alone in a locked room unless they are married or related by blood. In so doing, they maintain a sensitivity that others have lost. And for this they are to be envied.

Not long ago, I read an article about a young man who had recently begun to follow this way of life. When the journalist asked him about his social life, he said that since he was not yet contemplating marriage, he did not date.

"Isn't that kind of weird?" she asked. "Doesn't it seem unhealthy?"

The student explained, "The way I feel now, just to brush against a woman's finger would be exciting. I don't feel deprived—it's the friends I left behind in college who are deprived. I feel sorry for them. They're the ones who are missing out on something, not me."

This is a lucky man. This is a young man for whom the wonder and mystery and excitement of sexuality is a living reality.

In the synagogues of traditional Jews, men and women sit separately. People often ask me, "Why do you do this? Do you have to have a wall between you to keep you from sinning? Can't you keep your mind on your prayers without it?"

The purpose of the separation between men and women is not to prevent adultery in the aisles. Yes, at the lowest level, this separation will keep sin from occurring. But the answer is deeper than that. The purpose of the separation in the synagogue isn't to handcuff people to keep them from misbehaving. The purpose is to preserve and protect our sense of sexuality, which we can squander if we're not careful.

According to Jewish tradition, a male guest is not supposed to look upon the bride at her wedding. To prevent him from losing control and becoming a werewolf in the middle of the ceremony? No, the reason is more subtle: he might be moved to sexual feelings that are not appropriate. And experiencing sexuality when it's not appropriate can be damaging and deadening.

The story is told that, soon after the steamboat was invented, a captain brought his boat down the river and stopped at one of the small villages in Europe to show it off. He was fascinated by his new toy, and tried repeatedly to impress the simple peasants with the loud boom of his foghorn.

Over and over again, the captain stoked the engines, got up a big head of steam, and sounded the horn. But when it came time to show how the boat ran, it wouldn't budge. He had used up all his steam on the foghorn. "He had whistled his steam right out," the storytellers used to say.

And so it is with our sexuality. If we waste our energy wherever we go, we're left without any when we need it. If we are sexual when it doesn't count, we will have no steam left when it does.

Every interaction between male and female should be recognized as a potentially sexual encounter. If the door is locked and a man and a woman find themselves alone in the room, it becomes a sexual event. When we find ourselves in such a situation, we have to acknowledge that we are involved in a male-female relationship. Did we intend to become involved in that way? If not, why are we there?

If we feel a sexual attraction to someone we may not be sexually involved with, whatever the circumstances—whether it's a male physician with female patients, or a female therapist with male patients, or a male professor with female students—we have to put some distance between ourselves. But we cannot pretend we are not in a potentially sexual relationship.

It is preferable that a man and a woman who are not married to one another, and are not members of the same family avoid being alone together in a closed room. They should avoid talking about intimate subjects. This doesn't mean they shouldn't be friends or co-workers. But they need to take into consideration that whenever a man and a woman have a friendship or a working relationship, it will have a potentially sexual component. For this reason they should follow certain precautions.

They can be friends, they can work side by side, but they shouldn't go off alone on a canoe trip. They can discuss politics, art, business, or sports but should avoid topics that may initiate or strengthen feelings of sexuality. If their feelings get out of hand, they should break it off immediately. They should say, "Wait a minute, we can't do this. Sorry." In other words, they should do something to prevent sexual feelings when no sexual event ought to be taking place.

It's really very simple. By not arousing the attraction in the first place, by avoiding sexual stimulation to which they would have to say "no," they won't have to say "no" too often, and they won't kill their ability to respond.

Chapter 16
Why Doesn't Anyone Blush Anymore? Reclaiming Intimacy, Modesty, and Sexuality

There was once a wealthy man who had an interesting custom. His home was always open, and he would invite the poor people of his village to eat with him. He would ring a tiny crystal bell, a servant would appear with food, and they would all eat a fine meal. At the end of every meal, he would lay out his finest silverware and utensils and invite each guest to choose from among them a gift to take home.

One day a poor man from a neighboring village received an invitation to the wealthy man's house. When it came time for this poor man to make his request, he didn't ask for the obvious things, like a goblet or a decanter. Instead he asked for the little crystal bell.

The wealthy man felt that it was a strange request, and not a very useful item for a poor man who had no servants of his own. Nevertheless, he gave the guest what he asked for.

The poor man returned to his own village, and the next day invited all of his neighbors to a feast at his house. He set out two long wooden tables, and sat down to wait for his guests with great anticipation. The guests arrived, curious to know how such a poor man could expect to feed so many people. When the last person had arrived, the poor man removed the crystal bell from his pocket and made a great ceremony of ringing it.

Everyone waited. Nothing happened. He rang it again. Still nothing happened. He rang it loudly and insistently. But no servants appeared, no platters of food arrived, nothing. The poor man was humiliated. Red with indignation, he left his bewildered guests and ran all the way back to the wealthy man's house.

"You tricked me!" he cried. "You switched bells on me. You didn't give me your bell."

"Of course I did," said the wealthy man. "I gave you the very same bell that I used yesterday to summon my servants."

The poor man was livid with rage. "Why, then," he demanded, "did no one appear when I rang the bell?"

In our relationships, we are like the poor man. We ring the bell and nothing happens. Then we wonder: Who switched the bell on us?

Marriage used to be so simple: When a man and a woman got married, they rang the bell and the bell worked. Two people would meet each other. And if they liked each other, they got married. Once they got married, they stayed married. Our grandparents did it, our great-grandparents did it, even people who weren't very bright did it, and it worked. All sorts of people used to get married, the marriages were warm and close, and they lasted. Obviously, it didn't take much talent to make a successful marriage!

But today, when we ring the bell of marriage, it doesn't work the way it's supposed to. Somewhere along the line we made the mistake of assuming that such a wonderful relationship just happens automatically. We took it for granted. After all, people have been getting married for at least five thousand years. If they could do it, we ought to be able to do it, too. So we get married. And we wait for the warmth, the closeness, to arrive.

But nothing happens. Why isn't it working? What's missing?

What's missing is *intimacy,* the ability to share our dwelling place, that private place that exists within each of us that is personal, sacred, and deep. When a violation of the private place occurs, for whatever reason, our relationships become impersonal, profane, and shallow.

Until relatively recently, everyone knew what an intimate subject was. It was private, personal, and not for public consumption. If someone tried to talk about intimate feelings in conversation, everyone blushed and the subject was dropped. People understood their borders, they knew instinctively where to stop. But today we talk and talk about our need for intimacy, our lack of intimacy, our intimacy crisis—and we don't have the vaguest idea what we're talking about.

Sometimes the lack of intimacy in our lives manifests itself as a lack of depth in our relationships. We have friendships, marriages, children—and, on the surface, those relationships are fine. All the necessary details are there. We know what's right and what's wrong, and we go about our relationships with good intentions. Yet they lack passion, commitment, the deep sense of shared lives that characterized past generations. Everything seems a little flat. That flatness is the absence of the capacity for intimacy.

Once a little boy came home from school and asked his father, "Why did God create us with one nose and one mouth, but two eyes?"

His father thought about it, and after a while said to the boy, "God gave us two eyes, a right eye and a left eye. With the right eye we look at our friends; with our left eye we look at candies."

The little boy was asking an honest question and he deserved an honest answer. To say that we have one eye with which to look at our friends and the other eye to look at candies doesn't seem to answer the question. But the boy understood the father's answer and was satisfied.

Let's look a little closer. What would happen if we had only one eye? We would see height and we would see width, but we wouldn't be able to see depth. Everything would look a little flat.

We see in three dimensions because we have two eyes. With two eyes, we can see shallow or deep, near or far.

So what the father said to his son was not off the subject; it was the true answer to the question. He was merely wording his answer so that a child could understand. The reason we have two eyes is to discern the difference between shallow and deep. For a child, a candy is an example of shallow; a friend is deep.

The ability to penetrate past the surface, to have depth in our lives, to live in the richness of three dimensions, is probably the ultimate challenge that faces our generation. But instead of taking up the challenge, we surrender without a fight.

In the old days, a couple had to have very severe problems in order to get divorced. Having lost their affection for each other, they were consumed with hatred and friction. They had to get divorced; they had no choice. Today we find divorces that are polite and antiseptic—no bloodshed, no anger, no really serious complaints, no grief over the loss of an important relationship. Just "drifting apart."

Such a couple goes to a marriage counselor and says, "We want to get divorced."

"Why do you want to get divorced?" the counselor asks. "How can you get divorced after five years of marriage?"

"Well," they say, "there was never any intimacy between us."

This couple has been married for five years. They have shared the most intimate thoughts and activities. Yet they can turn around and say, "You know, we don't even feel married. No hard feelings, but we want a divorce. We have nothing against each other, but we're looking elsewhere for an intimate relationship."

How can that be? How did this happen to us?

At the beginning of time, when human beings made mistakes, if they misunderstood an aspect of their lives, if things went wrong, they assumed that the problem was religious. Maybe they were worshiping the wrong god, maybe they had omitted an important ritual, maybe they had offended their god in some way. The moral challenge of those days was to discover God.

According to the mystics, however, there is such a thing as the "evil inclination," whose role is to balance the powers of good and evil in the world so that human beings can have freedom of choice. In those days the evil inclination was devoted to confusing the issue about who God was. Because of this, the earliest people were often idolatrous. On the other hand, although they may have worshiped the wrong deity, they didn't have any problems with intimacy. They didn't question their roles as men or women, and they knew and respected the boundaries of each other's private space.

Today our problems are not so much with spirituality, but with the most tangible, the most earthy, the most personal aspects of our lives. The "evil inclination," as we know it, tries to confuse the physical aspect of our lives, interfering with our ability to act. Whereas the ancients struggled to understand the needs of their souls, we have to struggle to understand the needs of our bodies. Our moral challenge is to serve God through good deeds, with our hands, our feet, our mouths, our bodies. Accordingly, our difficulty is with intimacy, with the physical part of our lives.

Intimacy is a delicate ability. Like sexuality, the ability to be intimate and the ways of being intimate have to be protected and cultivated. In life as God intended it, intimacy has to be nurtured, preserved, and maintained. The tool the Bible gives us for this task is modesty: the border that protects our dwelling place.

For example, in many cultures throughout history, women have covered their hair. Was this meant to make them less attractive? If so, it didn't work. The head covering itself became attractive. The purpose must have been to conceal what was intimate.

There is no virtue in being unattractive. On the contrary, to be beautiful, to be attractive, to be impressive, is a virtue, especially in marriage.

The biblical woman who dressed modestly did so not to be less attractive, but to preserve and protect something fragile and easily lost: her ability to be intimate with her husband, which enriched both their lives.

It's part of our loss of understanding of what is intimate and what is not that we can no longer tell the difference between what is attractive and what is intimate. We can no longer appreciate that a garment is not intimate. But it was clear to the ancient sages that while a garment may bring compliments and attract attention, it doesn't evoke intimate feelings, either in the person who sees it or in the person who wears it—particularly in the person who wears it.

It's like the old question, "Do you lock your house to keep people out, or to protect what's inside?" Should a person act modestly and dress modestly in order to prevent intrusion from outside, undesirable things from happening, or to preserve and maintain what is inside: the delicate and sensitive ability to have and maintain an intimate relationship?

Many things are nice and attractive—we like clothes, we like fine art, we enjoy good food. But these things are not intimate; they don't touch that part of us that says, "This is who I am." Other things, however, do evoke intimate responses—our deepest feelings of love, the passionate expression of our sexuality, the revelation of our souls—and those things belong within the framework of marriage.

God's message to us is clear: A married woman needs to reserve her intimacy for her husband, and a married man needs to reserve his intimacy for his wife. That can only occur within the protective framework of modesty. Profoundly and significantly, this biblical wisdom helps us protect our innate and precious abilities from becoming dulled, corrupted, and lost.

Modesty is there to preserve intimacy, not to prevent sin. Modesty wasn't made for the person who wants to sin, just as laws were not made for people who want to commit crimes. Modesty has to do with something much more subtle: preserving our third dimension, the ability to have a deep, intimate relationship.

If we want to sin, we can sin, no matter how modestly dressed we are. The Puritans and Victorians were overdressed and extremely modest, but it didn't minimize their sinning. It simply made it more cumbersome. They had to be a little more determined, but they managed to sin.

The purpose of modesty is not to hide ourselves from view; the purpose of modesty is to preserve our intimacy. Even between a husband and wife, there is still a need for modesty. And especially between husband and wife, the intimacy has to be nurtured and protected. If the marriage is going to last a lifetime, the way it's supposed to, husband and wife must work together to preserve the intimacy.

When God said, "Be modest," He was telling us, "Preserve and protect your intimacy. It's a delicate and precious capacity. And if you don't take care of it, you'll lose it." When all is said and done, modesty preserves the wealth behind the ringing of the bell.

Modesty today will cause the ringing of the bell to have the effect we are searching for, the effect our grandparents and great-grandparents had when they rang the bell: Intimacy and Sexuality as God intended.

RABBI MANIS FRIEDMAN is available for lectures, family counseling and marriage workshops, and encounter-style weekends:

- ❏ I am interested in having Rabbi Friedman speak to my organization.
- ❏ I am interested in helping to bring Rabbi Friedman's TV show, TORAH FORUM, to my area.

Please send me information about spending some time with Rabbi Friedman:

at BAIS CHANA INSTITUTE, Minnesota

- ❏ for women   ❏ for men
- ❏ for couples   ❏ for teenage women

or at retreats

- ❏ at a lakeside resort
- ❏ canoeing and fishing in the Boundary Waters
- ❏ exploring the wilds of Costa Rica

Please put me on your mailing list:

- ❏ for Rabbi Friedman's speaking tour schedule
- ❏ for audiotapes by Rabbi Friedman
- ❏ for videotapes by Rabbi Friedman

❏ Please accept my tax-deductible contribution to the COMMUNITY EDUCATION ORGANIZATION (CEO).

Name: _____

Address: _____

Phone Day/Night:_____   _____

Fax:_____

Mail to: COMMUNITY EDUCATION ORGANIZATION, 3208 W. Lake Street, Suite 770, Minneapolis, MN 55416. or **Fax to:** (612) 922-8360.

RABBI MANIS FRIEDMAN is available for lectures, family counseling and marriage workshops, and encounter-style weekends:

- ❏ I am interested in having Rabbi Friedman speak to my organization.
- ❏ I am interested in helping to bring Rabbi Friedman's TV show, TORAH FORUM, to my area.

Please send me information about spending some time with Rabbi Friedman:

at BAIS CHANA INSTITUTE, Minnesota

- ❏ for women ❏ for men
- ❏ for couples ❏ for teenage women

or at retreats

- ❏ at a lakeside resort
- ❏ canoeing and fishing in the Boundary Waters
- ❏ exploring the wilds of Costa Rica

Please put me on your mailing list:

- ❏ for Rabbi Friedman's speaking tour schedule
- ❏ for audiotapes by Rabbi Friedman
- ❏ for videotapes by Rabbi Friedman

❏ Please accept my tax-deductible contribution to the COMMUNITY EDUCATION ORGANIZATION (CEO).

Name: ———————————————————————

Address: ——————————————————————

Phone Day/Night:————————————————

Fax:————————————————————————

Mail to: COMMUNITY EDUCATION ORGANIZATION, 3208 W. Lake Street, Suite 770, Minneapolis, MN 55416. or **Fax to:** (612) 922-8360.

RABBI MANIS FRIEDMAN is available for lectures, family counseling and marriage workshops, and encounter-style weekends:

    ❏ I am interested in having Rabbi Friedman speak to my organization.

    ❏ I am interested in helping to bring Rabbi Friedman's TV show, TORAH FORUM, to my area.

Please send me information about spending some time with Rabbi Friedman:

at BAIS CHANA INSTITUTE, Minnesota

    ❏ for women   ❏ for men

    ❏ for couples   ❏ for teenage women

or at retreats

    ❏ at a lakeside resort

    ❏ canoeing and fishing in the Boundary Waters

    ❏ exploring the wilds of Costa Rica

Please put me on your mailing list:

    ❏ for Rabbi Friedman's speaking tour schedule

    ❏ for audiotapes by Rabbi Friedman

    ❏ for videotapes by Rabbi Friedman

❏ Please accept my tax-deductible contribution to the COMMUNITY EDUCATION ORGANIZATION (CEO).

Name: ————————————————————

Address: ———————————————————

Phone Day/Night: ——————————————

Fax: —————————————————————

Mail to: COMMUNITY EDUCATION ORGANIZATION, 3208 W. Lake Street, Suite 770, Minneapolis, MN 55416. **or Fax to:** (612) 922-8360.